T
CLASSROOM
RESEARCHER

Using Applied Research to Meet Student Needs

Suzanne G. Houff

Rowman & Littlefield Education
Lanham, Maryland • Toronto • Plymouth, UK
2008

Published in the United States of America
by Rowman & Littlefield Education
A Division of Rowman & Littlefield Publishers, Inc.
A wholly owned subsidiary of The Rowman & Littlefield Publishing Group, Inc.
4501 Forbes Boulevard, Suite 200, Lanham, Maryland 20706
www.rowmaneducation.com

Estover Road
Plymouth PL6 7PY
United Kingdom

British Library Cataloguing in Publication Information Available

Library of Congress Cataloging-in-Publication Data
Houff, Suzanne G., 1953–
  The classroom researcher : using applied research to meet student needs /
Suzanne G. Houff.
    p. cm.
Includes bibliographical references.
ISBN-13: 978-1-57886-753-0 (cloth : alk. paper)
ISBN-10: 1-57886-753-3 (cloth : alk. paper)
ISBN-13: 978-1-57886-754-7 (pbk. : alk. paper)
ISBN-10: 1-57886-754-1 (pbk. : alk. paper)
  1. Education–Research. 2. Education–Research–Methodology. I. Title.
LB1028.H636 2008
370.7'2–dc22   2007039836

⊗™ The paper used in this publication meets the minimum requirements of
American National Standard for Information Sciences—Permanence of Paper
for Printed Library Materials, ANSI/NISO Z39.48-1992.
Manufactured in the United States of America.

CONTENTS

INTRODUCTION

This workbook is designed to provide you with an introduction to educational research and offer a guide to the applied research process. The term *applied research* is used to describe the process of strategically finding an answer or solution to an educational problem. This guide initiates you to the research process by guiding you through the identification of an educational problem or issue, the conducting and writing of a thorough literature review, and the development of an authentic application that addresses the problem.

By the time you complete the applied research process outlined in this workbook, you will be able to:

- Identify the purpose of research as it impacts decision-making and educational practices.
- Recognize various approaches to conducting educational research.
- Apply the APA format as it relates to writing a formal literature review.
- Critique scholarly literature to document research problems and solutions.
- Develop an effective problem statement.

- Develop a solution to an educational problem based on a thorough literature review.
- Validate your current practices.

With everything else that you need to do in the classroom, why would you want to take on research? Probably the main reason to become a classroom researcher classroom is that as a professional, you want to use the best practices to meet the needs of your students. To determine this, you need to become a reflective practitioner who strategically investigates what is most effective. Based on that knowledge, further practices can be developed.

Applied research can validate what you already know and practice as an effective teacher. By understanding and implementing research methodology, you can show how and why your teaching is improving classroom instruction and how it is meeting the needs of your students.

To provide a foundation for your research, you will first take a look at the purpose of educational research and some of the methodologies used by researchers.

2

BACKGROUND INFORMATION

Throughout the school day, you make important decisions regarding instruction. What do you base those decisions on? Intuition, beliefs, and common sense are helpful but in this age of accountability, they do not offer documented validity.

Intuition, beliefs, and common sense can be immediate. They can, however, be undependable and incomplete. For example, you might intuitively believe that your student, Laura, is missing semantic cues in her reading but a running record provides more accuracy and documentation.

You can back up intuition and common sense by comparing similar experiences and thoughts with colleagues. You might discuss the best classroom-management techniques with neighboring teachers and, based on their input, develop your own routine. However, it is possible for the majority to be wrong. It is also possible that what works for them might not be appropriate for you and your students.

Expert opinion can be valuable; however, the quality of information depends on the expert's credentials and how they received those credentials. If you use expert opinion as a basis for classroom decisions, do a thorough background check to determine the quality and validity of the opinion. Find out what research has been completed and documented by others in the field. Expert opinion is not infallible.

The scientific method can offer documentation and proof that supports what you believe. This process is a systematic strategy of testing ideas and problem solving. This objective thinking process identifies facts that can lead to an understanding of relationships. John Dewey (1938) suggested that the scientific method involve the following steps:

1. Clarify the main question inherent in the problem.
2. State a hypothesis (a possible answer to the question).
3. Collect, analyze, and interpret information related to the question and hypothesis.
4. Form conclusions derived from the information analyzed.
5. Use the conclusions to verify or reject the hypothesis. (Mertler, 2006, p. 6)

As you progress through the applied research process, you will see how the scientific method closely relates to your own research and application steps.

Understanding educational research provides you with the skill on which to base numerous educational decisions. Using research as a guide, you can make informed judgments that can be justified and authenticated. Staying current in the study of educational research allows you to understand trends, ask relevant questions, and perform your own studies to improve classroom instruction. The study of research is vital to you as a professional in that it allows you to incorporate the most effective instructional strategies.

APPROACHES

Educational research employs different methodologies, depending on the purpose of the research. The following is a brief look at experimental or non-experimental, qualitative or quantitative types of research.

EXPERIMENTAL AND NON-EXPERIMENTAL

Experimental research uses data to compare the effectiveness of two contrasting ideas or situations (variables) by measuring the effect of the independent variable on the dependent variable to determine a relationship. Random samples are used. Statistics are performed to determine the level of significance in the results. This analysis can indicate probability. In other words, statistics can show if the effects are "true effects" because of the manipulation of the independent variable or if the result happened by chance.

---

dependent variable The "effect" variable is a cause–effect relationship. For example, a new strategy (the independent variable) is being used to improve reading comprehension (the dependent variable).

independent variable The causative variable in a cause–effect relationship. The independent variable is intentionally manipulated, when possible, to observe the effects it might bring about in the dependent variable.

level of significance The odds conventionally used by researchers in tests of significance. Those odds are set at 5 chance recurrences of the finding out of 100 repetitions, and 1 chance recurrence of the finding out of 100 repetitions, on average (the 0.01 probability or significance level).

random samples A group drawn from the population with every member of the population having an equal chance of being selected (Mertle, 2005).

Example: Let's say you wanted to research the following question:

Do the math scores of students diagnosed with LD improve when these students receive math instruction in an inclusion classroom?

The purpose of the study is to test the effect of the inclusion classroom on math scores. Two randomly selected groups of children with LD are formed. One group participates in math instruction in an inclusion classroom and one does not. Inclusion classrooms are manipulated and, therefore, are the independent variable. The math scores are influenced by the inclusion classroom use or lack of use; therefore, the scores are the dependent variable.

A random sample is used and statistics performed to determine if there is a significant difference in the math scores when students with LD are placed in inclusion classrooms for math instruction.

Application of the statistical results can only be as effective as the research performance. Issues of validity and reliability come into play. *Valid research* means that your data measure what you say the data is measuring. If the research is reliable, it can be reproduced. The following questions check for validity and reliability:

Is your sample large enough and truly random? In other words, did all members of the population have the same chance at being in the selected group?

- Did the test measure what you thought it was measuring?
- Did you use the correct statistical procedures?
- Are your conclusions supported by the evidence you have gathered?

Although experimental research can be the most persuasive, it is very difficult and rarely performed in education because of the influence of outside variables.

Non-experimental research is much more likely to take place in the education arena. With non-experimental research, there is no direct manipulation of the independent variable.

Using the same example as before, let's look at a non-experimental design.

Do the math scores of students diagnosed as LD improve when the students receive math instruction in an inclusion classroom?

In this scenario, you use one group of students with LD. You give a pretest, provide math instruction in an inclusion classroom, and give a post test. This process is repeated without inclusion, provided so that the results can be compared. The independent variable in this situation is the group of students with LD. Because the independent variable cannot be manipulated, this is a non-experimental design.

QUALITATIVE AND QUANTITATIVE

Qualitative research produces narrative data that are verbally and inductively analyzed by looking for patterns and themes and determining what the data are suggesting. The data can be analyzed by grouping themes in a manner that makes sense and correlates with the literature. The natural setting is the direct source of data. Researchers are concerned with the process as well as the product.

The following questions are example of issues a researcher might address for a qualitative study:

- How do successful history teachers teach?
- What happens when a new inclusion program is instituted in an elementary school?

- What activities take place in classrooms that use cooperative learning?
- What is family life like for a child with autism?

Qualitative techniques to gather data can include observation, interview, survey, or focus groups (Johnson & Christensen, 2006):

> **observation** Unobtrusive watching of behavioral patterns of people.
>
> **interview** A data-collection method where interviewer asks the interviewee questions.
>
> **survey research** A term applied to non-experimental research based on questionnaires or interviews.
>
> **focus groups** A moderator facilitates a discussion with a small group of people.
>
> http://www.southalabama.edu/coe/bset/johnson/dr_johnson/2glossary.htm#.

Quantitative research produces data that are collected in numerical form and statistically analyzed. This type of research uses a deductive logic. Deductive reasoning suggests that if the premises are correct, the conclusion is correct. For example: All oranges are juicy. This is an orange and therefore it must be juicy. Conclusions are drawn from a set of premises.

The following are examples of issues a researcher might address in a quantitative study:

- What are the three most effective strategies for secondary history teachers?
- Do the reading scores of fifth grade students improve when teachers use a scripted reading basal?
- Does the retention rate for multiplication tables increase when cooperative groups are used for instruction?
- Is there an increased divorce rate among parents with autistic children?

Educational research usually incorporates two of the labels discussed. The study is experimental and quantitative, non-experimental and quan-

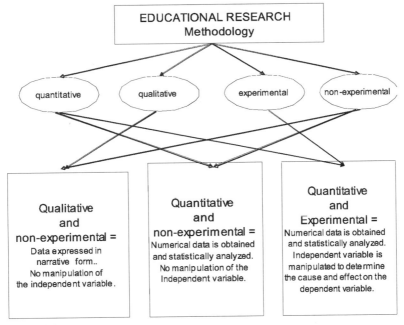

Figure 3.1.

titative, or non-experimental and qualitative. Educational research will never be experimental and qualitative. Why?

The following chart provides a visual of the methodologies reviewed.

EXERCISE 1: APPROACHES TO RESEARCH

To help you better understand and differentiate between the approaches to educational research, look at the following possible research studies. Determine if the proposal is qualitative or quantitative in design.

1. Ronald Huff wants to determine if there is a relationship between the ethnicity of a student and the type of reading genre preferred.
2. Linda Ware wants to determine which elementary learning experience was most significant to graduating seniors.

3. Marie Exum wonders if there is a correlation between the time of day she grades papers and the scores received.
4. Pam Chik wants to describe the metacognitive processes used by first graders in determining the meaning of a word in text.
5. Bruce Wayne is interested in understanding the affects of punishment as a motivator for his students.

ANSWERS

1. Quantitative. The purpose of this research is to establish a relationship between measured variables: genre and ethnicity.
2. Qualitative. Information will be collected in a social situation resulting in multiple "truths."
3. Quantitative. This is a study of the relationship between two variables.
4. Quantitative. The purpose of this research is to provide information regarding a specific reading process.
5. Qualitative. The goal of this study is to develop an understanding. There could be multiple realities within a social environment.

4

THE RESEARCH: GETTING FOCUSED

If you go to a dentist for a root canal, chances are, you want the doctor to use well-researched methods documented to be effective. You want the most current information regarding best practices for long-term effect and short-term discomfort. Your students deserve no less. Knowing how to find research and implement the documentation for classroom practices leads you to use the best methods to meet the needs of your students.

To prepare you for research and to illustrate how to use research to guide instruction, you will work through the process of identifying a problem, looking at quality research that has already been completed concerning that problem, and developing an instructional tool based on the research that you found.

ELEMENTARY EXAMPLE

Step 1: Let's say you are interested in developing a plan for classroom management that does not involve punishment. That is your topic: discipline without punishment.

Step 2: Now you focus it into a question: How can I develop a classroom discipline plan that does not involve punishment?

Step 3: In order to answer that question, you need to look at the lit-
          erature to find out:
              The advantages of not using punishment to maintain con-
          trol in the classroom. Is it worthwhile to use? Why should you
          consider eliminating punishment?
              The process to develop and implement a management pro-
          gram that does not involve punishment. What do you need to
          do? How will the program look?
              Once you have conducted a thorough literature search to
          identify the advantages of a non-punishment management
          approach, you are able to support its use in your classroom.
          The process of development still needs to be addressed to en-
          sure that you develop a successful program.
Step 4: You develop a management program that reflects what you
          found in your literature review. For example, in the scenario
          of the discipline without punishment, you develop the man-
          agement plan and implement it in your classroom. Figure 4.1
          shows an example of how this process might look in an or-
          ganizing framework.

MIDDLE SCHOOL EXAMPLE

Step 1: Let's say you are interested in using picture books with mid-
          dle school students. That is your topic: middle school stu-
          dents and picture books.
Step 2: Now you focus it into a question: How can I use picture
          books with my seventh grade students?
Step 3: In order to answer that question, you need to look at the lit-
          erature to find out characteristics of good picture books to
          use with adolescents and strategies to effectively use the pic-
          ture books with middle school students.
              Once you have conducted a thorough literature search to
          identify the characteristics and the strategies, you can then
          write your literature review addressing these issues and syn-
          thesizing what the research suggests.
Step 4: You develop a product that reflects what you found in your
          literature review. For example, in the scenario of the picture

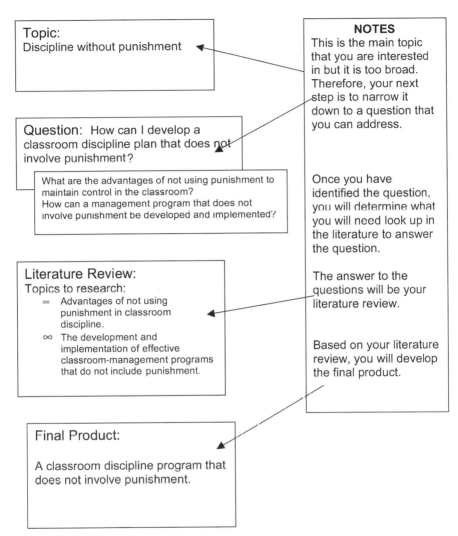

Figure 4.1.

books and middle school students, you might develop an annotated bibliography of quality picture books to use with middle school students. In addition to this bibliography, you would also provide lesson plans on strategies to use the books for effective instruction.

Figure 4.2 is an example of how this process might look in an organizing framework.

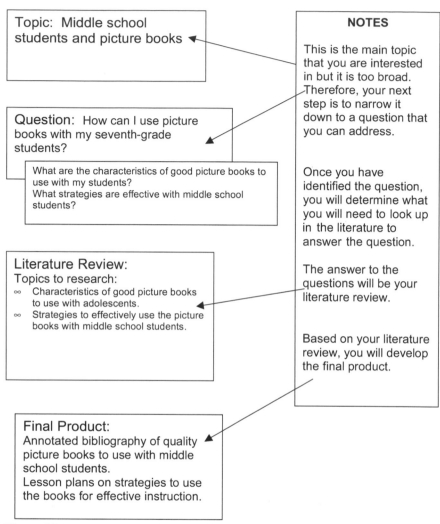

Figure 4.2.

SECONDARY EXAMPLE

Step 1: Let's say you are interested in using learning centers in an 11th grade English class. That is your topic: secondary learning centers

Step 2: Now you focus it into a question: How can learning centers be developed for the secondary classroom.

Step 3: In order to answer that question, you look at the literature to find out:
- The effectiveness and appropriateness of learning centers in the secondary classroom.
- The characteristics of an effective learning center for the secondary classroom.

You might find out that learning centers have not been effective in secondary classrooms. Therefore, you will know not to waste your time on this project. But, you might find that they have been very successful. Now you can validate their use in your own classroom and move on to find out how to develop an effective product.

Step 4: You develop a product that reflects what you found in your literature review. For example, in the scenario of the learning centers, you will use the information that you found to develop a learning center in your classroom.

Figure 4.3 shows how this process might look in an organizing framework.

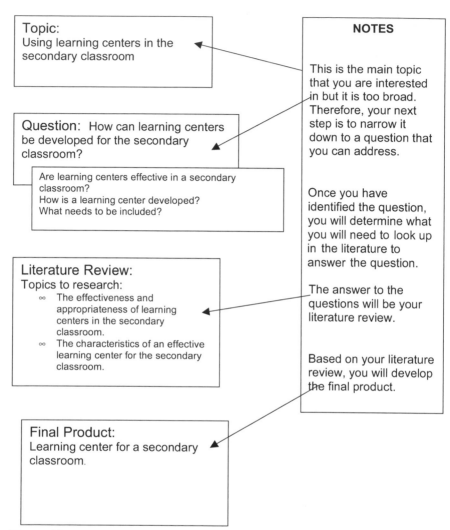

Topic:
Using learning centers in the secondary classroom

Question: How can learning centers be developed for the secondary classroom?

Are learning centers effective in a secondary classroom?
How is a learning center developed?
What needs to be included?

Literature Review:
Topics to research:
- ∞ The effectiveness and appropriateness of learning centers in the secondary classroom.
- ∞ The characteristics of an effective learning center for the secondary classroom.

Final Product:
Learning center for a secondary classroom.

NOTES

This is the main topic that you are interested in but it is too broad. Therefore, your next step is to narrow it down to a question that you can address.

Once you have identified the question, you will determine what you will need to look up in the literature to answer the question.

The answer to the questions will be your literature review.

Based on your literature review, you will develop the final product.

Figure 4.3.

CHOOSING A TOPIC: STEP I

What are some educational concerns or questions that you have? What are some of the student needs you see in the classroom?

How can you find the answers to your questions?

Start with a general educational area that interests you. Your topic should be a current issue that is relevant to you and to the field of education.

To help you get started, the following list offers education topics for you to brainstorm.

differentiation	ELL	content reading
best practices	technology	character education
classroom management	homework	student accountability
creative arts	thematic units	parental involvement
motivation	evaluation	classroom climate

As you brainstorm these additional topics, realize that the large topics are much too broad to research. They must be broken down into manageable subtopics from which a researchable question can be developed.

For example, using the topic of assessment, figure 5.1 shows how the topic is broken down into subtopics.

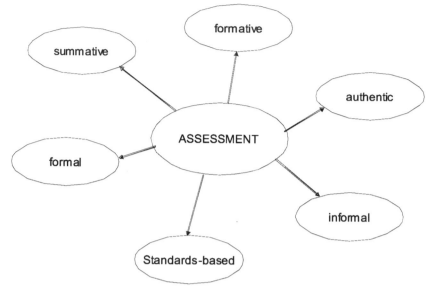

Figure 5.1.

Select one of the topics that you would like to further investigate. Using the topic organizer found in Appendix B, brainstorm possible subtopics.

Once you have decided on a topic, begin organizing your research and product by filling in the topic in the Appendix A framework.

6

DEVELOPING A PROBLEM
STATEMENT AND QUESTION

Once you have identified your topic, you need to narrow the focus with specific questions. You might ask yourself the following:

- Is my topic narrow enough to focus my literature review or is it so broad that it will expand in too many directions?
- Can I realistically use the information that I gain?
- Am I addressing a real problem? Will there be research to address my concerns?
- How can I narrow my topic to address a specific question?

In other words, ask yourself, "What do I really want to know about this topic? "What do I need to find out about this topic that will help me in the classroom?"

The answer to these questions explain the purpose of your study and gives direction to your literature review.

Look at the following problem statement:

Students in my second grade class are scoring low on the reading test.

Obviously, this is a problem but the statement is too vague to be addressed. Does this teacher mean all of the students? What is a low score? Is it a standardized reading test?

It might be better stated as:

Forty-three percent of my second grade ESOL students do not have the vocabulary skills to pass the state-mandated reading test.

This statement identifies and quantifies the problem. It is written clearly so that the researcher can determine that the literature review needs to address the topic of ESOL and vocabulary skills. More specifically, the researcher now needs to investigate how to identify what skills are needed and what strategies best improve vocabulary skills for the ESOL student. The following research question develops:

What strategies are most effective in helping ESOL students develop vocabulary skills?

EXERCISE 2: PART A

Read the following statements. What questions come to mind when you read these problems? What needs to added, deleted, or revised? Rewrite each statement to provide a better-stated problem.

- Rising high school seniors have not been prepared for the writing challenges of senior level work.
- Many people believe that employers will not hire an individual with an online degree if there is an equal candidate with a traditional degree. Because of this belief, many are hesitant to pursue an online degree.
- Men and women who drop out of school are considered to be functionally illiterate.
- Peer influence can negatively affect academic success of high school students.
- Newly certified and/or junior instructors within the Technical Skills curricula have inadequate basic instructional skills, particularly in the areas of questioning techniques, checking for understanding, and interactive teaching methods.
- Inclusion is not being implemented correctly in many schools.

- Students with learning disabilities do not achieve the same academic level as those without disabilities in secondary and postsecondary education.
- Students with language barriers are reading and comprehending below grade level.
- Teachers in School X are not using technology effectively on a daily basis with their students.

EXERCISE 2: PART B

Using your problem statements, develop a question that addresses each of the problems.

You have brainstormed major educational topics and narrowed the research by identifying subtopics. Now, based on those subtopics, use the topics organizer you started earlier to develop questions for investigation.

The completed example in figure 6.1 uses the assessment topic to illustrate the process.

Look at the organizer you completed. Which questions interest you the most? Which question do you feel you could address to produce a useful application? Be sure that the question is one in which the answer will provide you with the information that will lead to improved instruction.

You now have your topic and the question. What do you need to know to answer that question? The answer to this is the content for your literature review.

What classroom tool can be developed based on the content of your literature review?

Using your topic and question in the framework, write out the questions that you need to answer. Identify the issues to research for the literature review and decide on a final product.

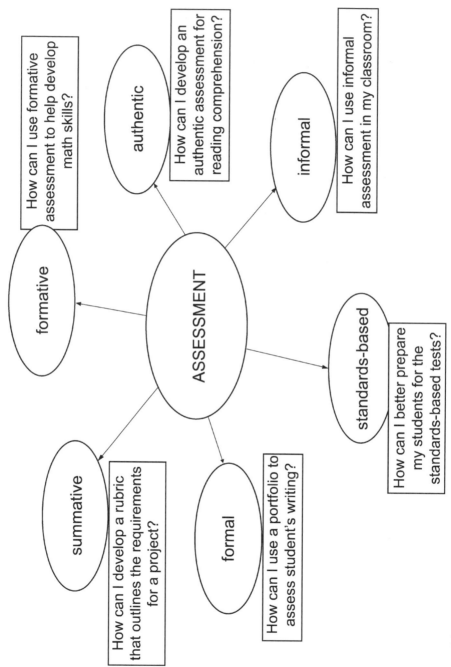

Figure 6.1.

LOCATING SOURCES

Jami L. Bryan, Library Manager, College of Graduate and Professional Studies, University of Mary Washington

THE VARIETY OF EDUCATIONAL RESEARCH

Research on education topics comes from a wide variety of authors. Many articles and books are written by practitioners in the field (i.e., teachers and administrators) or by faculty or researchers at colleges and universities. Federal, state, and local government agencies also sponsor research and publish reports and statistics on education topics. Countless organizations provide information on education issues as well. As the creators of educational research vary, so do their methods of publication. Research can be published as journal, newspaper, or magazine articles; books; theses; government documents; organization newsletters or reports; conference proceedings; websites; and even blogs.

Because so much information is available from authors with differing reasons for pursuing and publishing their research, it is crucial to evaluate every source. In evaluating a source, you should keep in mind the credentials of the creator or author, as well as their authority on the topic, and any point of view or agenda that could affect their findings. As discussed in Chapter 1, another way of evaluating a source is to examine the author's methodology and determine whether their research was quantitative or qualitative and experimental or nonexperimental.

You can also evaluate many sources based on the editorial processes under which they are published. One significant distinction is whether or not the publication is considered to be popular or scholarly. Popular publications include material that can be understood by a general audience. Scholarly publications include material written by experts in a field and require prior knowledge of the topic to be understood. Both popular and scholarly publications undergo editorial review before publishing, but many scholarly publications also put the article or report through a peer-review process. Peer-reviewed articles are vetted for authority, accuracy, and sound methodology by experts, the author's peers in the field, prior to being accepted for publishing.

The distinction between popular and scholarly is not always clear or easy to determine. A particular area of confusion, especially in education research, involves trade publications. Although trade publications appeal to an audience with a specific field of interest, such as K–12 teaching or literacy, they are still considered to be popular sources—a reader of a trade magazine might have an *interest* in and experience with a particular topic, but they do not need any *expert knowledge* of the topic to understand the articles in that magazine (table 7.1).

The popular vs. scholarly distinction best applies to periodical publications, such as journals and magazines, but it can also be applied to other types of sources as well. Books undergo editorial review before publishing. Theses and conference proceedings are submitted to a form of review by faculty or peers. Organization reports or publications might go through an editorial review, but the review could be slanted by the organization's mission. Government publications are generally considered to be authoritative because of the unbiased or apolitical nature of government agencies.

Table 7.1. Examples of Sources

Popular Sources	Scholarly Sources
○ Mailbox	○ Childhood Education
○ Instructor	○ Reading Research Journal
○ Teacher Magazine	○ Teaching Exceptional Children
○ Education Week	○ American Educational Research Journal
○ Gifted Child Today	○ Educational Theory
○ Arts and Activities	○ International Journal of Bilingual Education and Bilingualism
○ Education Digest	○ Harvard Educational Review

Questions you may want to ask when evaluating a source:
Based on the creator/author:

- Does the author have expertise in the field in which they are writing?
- Is the author associated with an organization, academic institution, or government agency?
- How might the author's affiliations slant his or her findings?

Based on the method of publication:

- Was this published by a reputable publisher?
- Has it undergone an editorial or peer-review process?

Based on the content:

- What is the methodology behind the research? Are the methods sound?
- Are the findings supported by facts, experiment, observation, or are they merely opinion?
- Are you being given the full story or just one side?

Based on your other research:

- How do the findings of this source compare to the other sources you have found?
- Is the author or work cited in other authoritative sources?

FINDING EDUCATIONAL RESEARCH

So how do you find a wealth of quality information on educational topics? Myriad resources are available to help you discover and access what has been written on your topic of interest.

Using Library Resources

Libraries offer several resources that will be invaluable to your research. Although your local public library is a good place to begin, you might also want to gain access to libraries with more specific, research-oriented collections, such as a university or college library. You might find that you are able to use a university or college library's collections and resources based on your alumni or continuing education status. Many academic libraries also grant special access to school teachers and staff. Even if you aren't granted borrowing privileges at the local university library, you might still be able to use their collections and resources—most libraries at public academic institutions are open to the general public and will allow you to use their books and periodicals within the library. Your school's library might also provide access to resources appropriate for your professional research.

Encyclopedias   One of the best sources for beginning your research is an encyclopedia. Most libraries offer access to both general and subject-specific encyclopedias in their reference sections. An encyclopedia might seem like too elementary a source when conducting research for professional use, but these reference works can be a great starting point. You could use an encyclopedia entry to:

- Determine the history and major players of an issue.
- Help narrow your focus to a particular aspect of your topic.
- Discover related topics or other areas of research to explore.
- Familiarize yourself with the "vocabulary" or jargon of the topic or field.

Further, many encyclopedia entries include bibliographies or reference lists that can lead you to sources on your topic.

Library Catalogs   A library's catalog will tell you what materials are available on your topic in that library or library system. Gone are the days of card catalogs; most libraries have online catalogs, many of which can be searched remotely from your home or office. Online catalogs are often accessed from the library's website and allow you to search for materials by title, author, and subject.

You can search a library catalog for citation and availability information for the books the library holds in its collections. Catalogs might also include information about the government documents or theses held at the library. Library catalogs will usually include information about the library's periodical subscriptions also. You should be able to search for the title of the magazine, newspaper, or journal you want in the library's catalog and find out if the library holds a copy of that periodical for the date or issue you need. It is important to note that library catalogs do not include any information about the authors or articles published in periodicals. Catalogs only provide basic information about the periodical title (title, publisher, place of publication) and about the library's subscription to that title (the dates and issues for which they have copies).

The citation and availability information you find for an item in a library catalog is called a *record*. Most library records include subject headings, which are the terms librarians have used to describe the main topics of the book or item. These terms usually come from a consistent vocabulary; books or periodicals covering the same topic will be described using the same term. For example, one book about the role of parents in education will not be described using a heading of "parent participation" while another book on the very same topic is described using "parent involvement"—they will both be described using only the same headings.

The vast majority of libraries use one of two vocabularies to describe their materials; public and school libraries tend to use the Sears List of Subject Headings, while academic libraries often use the Library of Congress Subject Headings (table 7.2). This has two very useful impacts on the researcher. First, if you can find one good item on your topic in a library catalog, you can use the subject headings assigned to that item as new search terms and find other similar items held at that library. Second, because most libraries use either Sears or Library of Congress terms, you will likely get good results in one library catalog using search terms based on subject headings found in another library's catalog.

Table 7.2.   Catalog Record That Uses Library of Congress Subject Headings

Author:	Hannell, Glynis.
Title:	Identifying children with special needs: checklists and action plans for teachers
Publication:	Thousand Oaks, Calif.: Corwin Press, c2006.
Subject:	Children with disabilities—Education.
Subject:	Needs assessment.
Subject:	Ability—Testing.
Location:	Stacks
Copy:	I
Status:	Available for Checkout

A search of your local public or academic library's catalog will likely lead you to some valuable resources. However, you can expand your search beyond your local collections by using Worldcat, http://www .worldcat.org, a website that allows you to explore the catalogs of more than 10,000 libraries in one search. Worldcat results look similar to the results you might see in a library's catalog, in that each record includes citation information. However, a Worldcat record also includes information about which libraries around the world own the item. You can often follow links from Worldcat directly to a library's catalog or to more information about that library.

Databases

As previously stated, a library catalog won't be able to tell you which articles in journals, magazines, or newspapers have been written on your topic. To find out what has been published on your topic in periodicals, you will need to use a database. Databases are online, searchable resources that compile or index information about the articles that have been published in periodicals. Most databases compile abstracts, or summaries, of the articles as well. Many even provide access to the full text of the articles, allowing users to print or e-mail the articles they need.

Much like online library catalogs, online databases are easily searchable by article title, periodical title, author, and subject. Most will also allow you to limit the results you receive from a search in several ways, including limiting by date or to peer-reviewed or scholarly periodicals (Fig. 7.1).

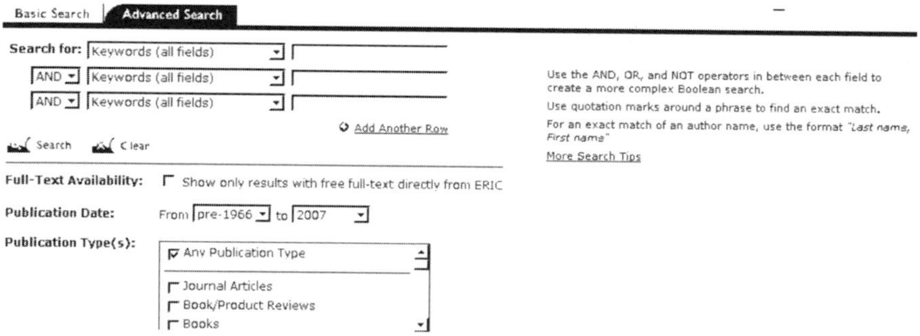

Figure 7.1.   Advanced search screen from the ERIC Database.

Although many databases cover different subject areas, databases tend to be subject-specific, meaning they only index periodicals on particular topics. Although most databases use subject headings (often referred to as *keywords* or *descriptors*), they rarely use the same vocabularies found in library catalogs. Databases might elect to use a vocabulary more relevant to a particular discipline or they might rely on authors or publishers to supply them with terms to describe an article.

One feature that is available in many databases is a "Subject Thesaurus." The thesaurus will allow you to compare your search terms to the list of subject headings used in that database. This extremely useful feature allows you to quickly determine the most appropriate search terms to use in searching that database. This is especially important in the field of education because some terms have been used to mean very different things in different time periods and places. An example is the term "gifted," which has been used by different authors to describe both the academically advanced *and* the developmentally challenged or disabled. Thus, without checking what the term "gifted" is referring to in any particular database, a search for that term could yield mixed results or results that are not on the topic you had hoped.

One of the most useful databases in the field of Education is ERIC, the Education Resources Information Center. ERIC includes citations dating back to 1966 and indexes books, conference and policy papers, reports, and journal articles from more than 600 journals. For many of the resources indexed in ERIC, the full-text of the item is available online in the database (you should check with your local library for assistance in obtaining the full-text of those items that are not available online). ERIC search features include a thesaurus and an Advanced Search with limits by publication type (Fig. 7.1). ERIC is provided by the U.S. Department of Education and is freely available on the Web at http://www.eric.ed.gov.

Although a very few databases are available on the Web for free or via a personal subscription, the vast majority are available through a library; libraries pay the subscription costs to databases so that their patrons can access these valuable resources. Most libraries make their databases available via their website so that patrons can use them from anywhere. However, nearly all libraries will require you to enter a library card number or other identifying information to prove that you are affiliated with their library, and thus allowed to access their subscription. Some libraries limit off-library access, so it might be necessary to use the database from computers in the library.

Making Use of Web Resources

Although library catalogs and databases will likely yield more relevant and appropriate results for your research, and depending on your topic and resource needs, you might want to search the Web for additional sources. Unless you are aware of specific sites of interest, one of the best ways to find out what is available on your topic is to use a search engine.

There are a variety of search engines, with the most well known being Google (http://www.google.com) and Yahoo (http://www.yahoo.com). Search engines work by "crawling" through the Web and capturing information from the sites and pages they are able to reach. As such, search engines mostly return results from the freely available Web and just skim the surface of what is available online. Search engines do not "crawl" protected resources, such as subscription databases, or other sites where content lies in enclosed systems, such as the records in a library catalog.

Database Search Tips

Use specific, rather than general, search terms or strategies

- Example: Use "literacy and reading skills and elementary" instead of "literacy."
- If available, try using the Advanced Search instead of the Basic Search; Advanced Search screens usually present more options for limiting your results.
- Use the Subject Thesaurus or Browse Subject Headings feature to verify you are using the most appropriate search terms for that database.
- Use the Help feature for search tips or to find out about the search options available in that particular database.

Because search engines do not reflect content from the "deep Web," they should not be relied upon as replacements for searching library catalogs or databases.

Further, although search engines do provide very user-friendly search screens, they do not assign subject headings to the sites they index. This can make finding resources relevant to your topic more difficult. Also, search engines typically order ("rank,") the sites they provide to you as results based on how many times your search terms appear on the page, as well as how often people click on any result or how many other sites link to that site. These latter factors mean that more popular sites appear at the top of results lists, while sites that are appropriate for professional research might not appear in the first 100 or even 10,000 results.

Similarly, finding relevant and appropriate results on the Web can be difficult because most search engines do not attempt to evaluate any of the pages they index for authority or accuracy. And because almost anyone can post almost anything they want to the Web, the vast majority of things posted online have not gone through any sort of editorial review. Some search engines have tried to overcome this problem by creating special engines that provide results only from scholarly or university sources. One such engine is Google Scholar, available at http://scholar.google.com/.

Beyond using special or subject-specific search engines, one way to make your search engine searches more effective is to use the available options for limiting your results. Many engines provide a link to an "Advanced Search" screen that offers you more search options than found on the basic search screen. A useful feature available at both Yahoo and Google is the ability to limit by domain. Domains, found in the address (URL) of a Web page, are an indicator of who is publishing a website: .com and .net in an address indicates commercial sites, while .gov is used for government sites, .org for organization sites, and .edu for sites owned by educational institutions. As such, it might be useful to limit your results to sites with .edu or .gov in the address.

Despite the many drawbacks to search engines, they can introduce you to resources that could be useful to your research. Still, it is especially crucial that you turn a critical eye to Web resources and evaluate those sources before using them in your research. In addition to the questions you should ask in evaluating any source, you might want to ask the following questions in evaluating a source you find on the Web:

- Can you determine who or what type of organization owns the site?
  ° Notice the URL (.edu, .org, .gov, .com, .net)
  ° Check for an "About Us" link
- When was the material written vs. when it was posted?
  ° Notice all dates on the site
- Is the author or work cited in other authoritative or print sources?

Getting to More Resources

Although catalogs, databases, and search engines will lead you to many valuable resources, you might find that you need more sources to round out your research. Two services offered at most libraries can assist you in locating further resources.

Interlibrary Loan   After searching online databases, search engines, and Worldcat, you will likely have a list of citations for books or articles that aren't available at your local library. Most libraries offer interlibrary loan (ILL), services to their patrons. A patron can make an interlibrary loan request for an item and the library will attempt to borrow or retrieve the item for the patron from another library. This is extremely useful because patrons aren't limited to their local collections, but can access materials held at libraries around the world. Some li-

---

Search Engine Search Tips

- Use very specific rather than general search terms or strategies.
- Look for an Advanced Search link and make use of the limiters available:
  ° Limit by domain (.gov, .edu, or .org)
  ° Limit by date
- Use the Help feature for search tips or to find out more about the search options available in that engine.

braries charge a fee for this service, often to cover postage on mailing the item between libraries.

Research Assistance   Probably the most useful service offered at libraries is research assistance. If you are struggling to find resources on your topic or are having difficulties using library resources or search engines, a librarian's knowledge of resources and research techniques can save you a lot of time and frustration. Libraries increasingly offer research assistance not only at their physical Reference or Information Desk, but also over the phone and online via e-mail and chat. Academic libraries also tend to have staff with subject specialties, so help from an Education or Social Sciences librarian with extensive experience in researching education topics might be available.

Tips for Finding More Resources

- If you find a useful book or article, search for other items by that author in a catalog or database.
- Check the reference list or bibliography of useful resources and search your library's catalog or place an Interlibrary Loan request for those books and articles.
- Check with any professional organizations you belong to and see if they offer access to periodicals or research tools through your membership.
- Ask colleagues, mentors, or other professionals to recommend books and periodicals.

8

READING THE LITERATURE

Reading published research articles can be confusing and time consuming because of the amount of information provided and the research terminology that is used.

For this applied research project, many of the research terms will not be applicable but the following glossary website sources will help you define unknown terms you encounter during your reading.

ONLINE GLOSSARY RESOURCES

http://www.southalabama.edu/coe/bset/johnson/dr_johnson/2glos sary.htm
http://ec.wmich.edu/glossary
http://oerl.sri.com/gloss.html
http://www.audiencedialogue.org/gloss-qual.html

The most efficient way to approach evaluating a journal article for your use is to skim/scan and summarize. Before reading, skim the article to identify the main ideas and the usefulness of the information. The title and introduction should clearly identify the subject matter of the article. The abstract provides an overall summary but you will need to scan the entire article for important details. After reading the article, summarize the information that is relevant to your research. Pay special attention to the conclusions portion of the article.

Ask yourself: "What conclusions can be drawn from the author's research?" "How can these conclusions be applied to my project?" "Will the article's list of references provide useful reference sources?"

The University of Southern California's guide to reading research articles provides useful guidelines to assist in the reading and deciphering of the information. Read the information regarding reading qualitative and quantitative research provided at the USC link. The questions provided at the site will guide you through determining if an article will be of value to your research.

http://www.usc.edu/hsc/ebnet/res/Guide%20to%20Reading%20 Research.pdf

Be sure to use peer-reviewed articles. Peer reviewed suggests that the article has been previewed by a panel of experts in the field before it was accepted for publication. Peer-reviewed articles indicate that the writing and the information is of quality and that it is relevant and authenticated.

HTTP://EN.WIKIPEDIA.ORG/WIKI/PEER_REVIEW

Peer review (known as *refereeing* in some academic fields) is a scholarly process used in the publication of manuscripts and in the awarding of funding for research. Publishers and funding agencies use peer review to select and to screen submissions. The process also forces authors to meet the standards of their discipline. Publications and awards that have not undergone peer review are likely to be regarded with suspicion by scholars and professionals in many fields.

ARTICLE EVALUATION EXERCISE

The purpose of this exercise is to help you glean the information from a quality research article (table 8.1). Locate a peer-reviewed article regarding a current study that relates to your topic and questions. Use the information from the article to answer the following questions.

Title of Article:
Author:
Title of Journal:
Copyright:

Table 8.1.

How does the article relate to your topic?	
What type of study was performed?	
Do you agree with the conclusions drawn? Why or why not?	
Is the population of the study similar to the population you will work with? How are they similar? How are they different?	
Are there any threats to the validity of the study? What are they?	
Does the author provide additional references or sources that could be useful? What are they?	
Based on the research you want to do, what question does this article answer?	
What is the answer to the question? How can you use the information provided in the article?	
What new information did you learn by reading this article?	
Does the information in the article support what you believe about the topic? Why or why not?	

LITERATURE REVIEW: STEP 3

The literature review is a documentation and validation of your work. By using documented research to develop your product, you can justify your teaching strategies and show how you meet the needs of student learning.

This critical survey of published works relates to your research and involves two phases:

- Reading and analyzing the publications (just like you did for the article evaluation exercise).
- Writing a report that synthesizes the most significant ideas and how they relate to your research.

This important report provides written documentation of the research that guides your instruction.

The literature review conveys to your reader what knowledge and ideas have been established on a topic. It is not a series of summaries of the articles you have read. Your literature review needs to provide relevant information regarding your topic and support the design of your final product.

As suggested by Leedy (1997), the literature review provides:

- a theoretical understanding of the subject of your research
- information from the ideas and research of others that may relate to your study
- additional viewpoints to consider
- other sources for information
- techniques and procedures to use in completing your project
- a list of factors that are considered important in determining the goals and outcomes of research

In preparation for the literature review, find at least three articles from educational journals that deal with your topic. They should address the issues you identified in your planning organizer. These articles should provide the information needed to develop the final product.

Use table 9.1 to list the articles you will use. This chart provides necessary information for the documentation of your support.

Table 9.1.

Author's Name	Date of Publication	Title of the Article	Name of the Journal	Volume of Journal Page Numbers of the Articles

The following websites provide additional information for the literature review.

http://www.utoronto.ca/litrev.html
http://owl.english.purdue.edu

STEP 3

For your literature review, you will write a synthesis of the research you have read concerning your topic. The review should be approximately five pages in length and contain at least three cited references. These are only guideline numbers for this applied project and do not reflect the appropriate number for a dissertation or thesis. The following organizer helps keep the focus on the issues. It will help keep track of where you found the answers and how they apply to your research.

Table 9.2.

Questions/Issues	Article 1	Article 2	Article 3

In the left hand column, write the issues or questions that you developed in the research organizer. Address each of these based on the information found in your journal articles.

Using the picture book scenario from the beginning of this guide, the information chart might look like this:

Table 9.3.

Questions	Article 1	Article 2	Article 3
	Perez, Theresa (2001) *Selecting Picture Books for Middle & Secondary Students* Falcon.jmu.edu/ ~ramseyil/secpict perez.html	Carr, Kathryn (2001). "Not just for the primary grades: A bibliography of picture books for secondary content teachers." *Journal of Adolescent and Adult Literacy.* October 45:2	International Reading Association (1999). *Adolescent literacy: A position statement*
What are the characteristics of good picture books to use with my students?	Illustrations expand and extend the story, can explore serious themes mature themes, illustrations create a mood.	Increase motivation Pictures and text work together Rich vocabulary Visually appealing	
What strategies are effective with middle school students?		Integration with the content areas Provide background information Vocabulary development	Questioning Synthesizing Vocabulary development Text organization Evaluating author's ideas

(10)

THE APPLICATION: STEP 4

The final product is the application of your literature review. After identifying an issue you want to research, you then review the literature to find out current information regarding that issue. Based on the information you gained, you will now develop a final product.

The following components should be included and clearly labeled in the final product. Binding is suggested in order that the project can be stored and used as a resource in your school.

Title Page
Table of Contents
Introduction
    Why you chose your topic, and your experience with the topic.
    How you plan to define and approach the topic.
Research Question or Questions/Problem
Literature Review
Conclusions
    How the research applies to your research question.
    How you plan to apply the research.
Application
    Your final product: curriculum units, professional development plan, Web page, instructional materials, etc.

(11)

SHARING THE RESEARCH

You have spent a great deal of time developing a literature review and final product. One purpose of research is to share the information with other professionals in the field. This sharing of information can take the form of local presentations, conference presentations, or published articles. You might want to meet with a school principal regarding sharing your material at an in-service meeting. Look under professional organizations and conferences in your field. Upcoming conferences will usually provide a form for possible presentation submissions. Use the following website to help locate an educational conference:

http://www.allconferences.com/Education/

Content-specific professional organizations announce conference and presentation opportunities. Table 11.1 provides a list of professional organizations and their websites.

Once your proposal has been accepted, you will need to plan your presentation.

Some guidelines to think about as you prepare include:

- Begin with an "attention getter." Grab the audience in the first 30 seconds.
- Keep major points simple and limited. It is a good idea to stick with five major points.

Table 11.1.

Organization	Website
National Council of Teachers of English	http://www.ncte.org
Teachers of English to Students of Other Languages	http://www.tesol.org
American Education Research Association	http://www.aera.net
National Middle School Association	http://www.nmsa.org
Phi Delta Kappa	http://www.pdkintl.org
American Association of School Administrators	http://www.aasa.org
American Library Association	http://www.ala.org
Association for Supervision and Curriculum Development	http://www.ascd.org
International Reading Association	http://www.reading.org
International Society for Technology in Education	http://www.iste.org
National Art Education Association	http://www.naea-reston.org
National Association of Elementary School Principals	http://www.naesp.org
National Association of Secondary School Principals	http://www.nassp.org
National Council for Geographic Education	http://www.ncge.org
National Council for Teachers of Math	http://www.nctm.org
National Association for Gifted Children	http://www.nage.org
National Science Teachers Association	http://www.nsta.org
National Council for the Social Studies	http://www.ncss.org
American Association of Physics Teachers	http://www.aapt.org
American Association of School Administrators	http://www.aasa.org

- Determine the most appropriate medium to present your information. Will you use straight lecture? PowerPoint? Slides?
- Keep "pacing" in mind. You do not want to go through the material too quickly and you do not want to drag the material out.
- "Stage fright" might be a consideration. It always seems more difficult to present in front of a group of your peers than a full room of children. The more practice you have at presenting in front of a group, the more comfortable you will become.

Lenny Laskowski (2002) offers the following suggestions for reducing anxiety when giving presentations:

- Become familiar with the room in which you are going to speak. Arrive early and familiarize yourself with the surroundings.
- Know to whom you will be speaking. Chat with a few people prior to your presentation.

- Know your material. Practice before the actual presentation. Be fully prepared and know exactly what you are talking about. Don't try to "wing it."
- Practice relaxation techniques.
- Visualize yourself speaking confidently in front of the group.
- Understand that people want you to succeed.
- Realize that usually your nervousness does not show, so do not apologize for being nervous. Turn the nervousness into positive energy.
- Focus on the message and not the audience.

ON YOUR OWN

Try taking the Arlington Associates Public Speaking Quiz. It will provide you with some tips for giving presentations. You can find this quiz at:

http://www.arlington-associates.co.uk/quiz2/index.html

PREPARE TO PUBLISH: USING APA

As you prepare to publish, you will first need to identify the appropriate audience for your research findings. The teachers or administrators will be interested in your research if they have a similar situation or concern. You can find journal publication standards by searching the Internet or by writing to the editor and requesting a copy of submission requirements.

Research reports and findings can take many different formats. You will first want to adhere to publication standards but if none are provided, the format used for your project is fine.

Provide an introduction that explains why you chose your topic and your prior experience in this area. Include how you plan to define and approach the topic and what research question or problem you are addressing. The literature review will provide the basic content of the manuscript. This will be followed by your conclusion and how the research applied to your question.

USING APA

American Psychological Association (APA) guidelines are essential to scholarly writing in the social sciences. APA specifics strict formats for scientific writing that provide an understandable and common "language" for educators. These guidelines include:

- In-text citations
- Paraphrases and quotations
- References
- Tables and figures
- Headings
- Abstracts
- Pagination

The following guideline—from the APA fifth edition manual—were compiled by Cheryl Hawkinson-Melkun and Pamela Denton, and the staff at the writing center of the College of Graduate and Professional Studies of the University of Mary Washington. This information offers an overview of how to use the APA guidelines.

APA GUIDELINES

General

Spacing   Double space all text, after each line in the title, headings, quotations, references, figure captions, and all parts of tables. (§5.03, p. 286)

Margins   Provide one-inch all the way around the page. (§5.04, p. 286)

Indentation   Indent the first line of each paragraph one-half inch (5 spaces). Set paragraph alignment to "align left"—this gives the paper a "ragged" right edge.

Direct Quotations (§§ 3.34, 5.13, pp. 117–292)   Avoid "dropping" quotations into the text. Anchor all quotations to the document with a lead-in or tag that links the quotation to your own writing. This "rule" applies to short (less than 40 words) *and* long (more than 40 words) quotations.

Use single quotation marks (' ') to enclose material that was enclosed in double quotations in your original source materials.

Enclose quotations of less than 40 words in quotations marks (" ") and blend them into the body of your text.

Quotations of more than 40 words (long quotations) are *not* enclosed in quotation marks. Instead, type long quotations in a double-spaced, stand-alone block, beginning on a new line. The entire block of the quotation is indented one-half inch (5 spaces) from the left margin; do not adjust your right margin. The following is an example of what a long quote will look like:

> In a word, the unaided consciousness must always involve man in the sort of stupidity of which evolution was guilty when she urged upon the dinosaurs the common-sense values of an armaments race. She inevitably realized her mistake a million years later and wiped them out. (Bateson, 1972, p. 146)

In-text Citations for Direct Quotations (§§3.39, p. 120)   The parenthetical citation for all quoted material must include the page number—using the notation "p." for a single page and "pp." for a quotation that spans more than one page.

Place parenthetical citations for quoted material immediately after the final set of quotation marks, before the punctuation mark. For example, "insert the quoted material" and then place the appropriate parenthetical citation (last name of author, year, p. xx).

The parenthetical citation for a direct quotation from a printed source should contain (author, year of publication/copyright, page number). If the quotation comes from a source that does not have page numbers, the citation should contain (author, year, and sufficient information to allow the reader to locate the quotation). Sufficient information would be (a) the paragraph number, if the paragraphs are numbered, or (b) the section heading and number of the paragraph in which the quotation is located, if such information is available. Examples for these citations are:

(Smith, 2005, ¶ 4)
(Smith, 2005, Conclusion section, ¶ 2)

If page numbers, paragraph numbers, or section headings are not available, this information can be omitted from the citation.

In-text Citations for Paraphrased Material (§3.39, p. 120)   Place the citation for paraphrased material at the end of the sentence, *before* the punctuation mark. Position the final punctuation mark for the sentence to the right of the closing parenthesis (author, year). Notice that page numbers are not required for paraphrased material but are recommended. The extent of indebtedness must be clear for all paraphrased or summarized material.

Punctuation and Citations   If a citation appears mid-sentence, it is not followed by any punctuation, except what may be required by the sentence. For example: Beginning of your sentence, "this is the quotation" (author, year, p. #) balance of your sentence follows the closing parenthesis.

If a citation appears at the end of a sentence, place the appropriate punctuation mark for the sentence after the closing parenthesis (author, year).

Unlike short quotations that appear in the body of the document (which are punctuated as previously described), long quotations are punctuated just as in their original text. The final punctuation mark is followed by the parenthetical citation; *no* punctuation follows the closing parenthesis for the citation.

Numbers (§§3.42–3.49)   The general rule under APA is that numbers 10 and greater are written in Arabic figures (10, 11, 12 . . .); numbers less than 10 are written out (one, two, three . . .). Exceptions to this rule are detailed in §§ 3.43–3.46 of the *Publication Manual of the American Psychological Association*. These exceptions include the following:

- §3.43 c. Spell out numbers of any size if they are the first word in a sentence, title, or heading (Try to re-write to avoid beginning with a number).
- §3.43 d. Common fractions are spelled out: **one-fifth of the class; two-thirds majority.**
- §3.43 e. Spell out numbers that are universally accepted as spelled out, for example: **the Twelve Apostles, the Fourth of July, the Ten Commandments.**
- §3.44. Combine figures and words when dealing with the following:
  - ○ rounded large numbers (beginning with millions) such as: **a budget of $2.5 billion, almost 3 million people.**
  - ○ back-to-back modifiers such as: **2 two-way interactions; twenty 10-year olds; the first 10 items.**

- When writing decimal fractions, insert a zero before the decimal point if the number is less than one (**0.23 inches**). However, do not insert a zero when discussing decimal fractions that cannot be greater than one (such as correlations and proportions).
- §3.49. When writing the plurals of numbers—whether the numbers or spelled out or written in figures—add an "s" or "es" without an apostrophe. For example: fours and sixes; 1950s, 10s, and 20s.

Appendixes (§3.90–3.93, pp. 205–207)   An appendix is the means by which writers can provide additional information without interrupting the flow of their document. A paper may contain more than one appendix.

If using only one appendix, label it Appendix; if using more than one appendix, each document in the appendix should be labeled with a capital letter (Appendix A, Appendix B, etc.) and given a brief, descriptive title. When referring to an appendix, use its label (Appendix A, etc.).

APA Reference List Guidelines

Reference List Entries (§§4.01–4.16, pp. 215–31)   The reference list is designed to help readers find source articles quickly and easily so that research can be replicated and data verified. Consequently, all sources cited in the body of the paper must appear on the reference list. Strict APA style dictates that if a source is not cited in the text of the document, it should not be included in the reference list. However, because Chapter 6 of the *Publication Manual of the American Psychological Association* (pp. 321–330) permits the inclusion of such source materials on the reference list.

Placement and Format of the Reference List   The reference list is placed after the last page of the text, before the appendix.

Entries in the reference list should be arranged in alphabetical order according to the author's last name or by article/book title if an author's name is not given. (§4.04, pp. 219–222)

Entries are double-spaced with a hanging indent, or, if following Chapter 6 guidelines, single-spaced and double-spaced between entries.

General Rules

Note: This chapter is not a complete listing of how to construct reference list entries. Additional information can be found in the APA manual. All examples used in this text are from the 5th edition of the *Publication Manual of the American Psychological Association.*

Authors   Invert authors' names, listing last names and initials for only the first six authors of a document. If a document has more than six authors, use "et al." after the sixth author's name. Use an ampersand (&) immediately preceding the final author's name unless the list contains seven or more authors.

Note: authors are listed in the order in which they are listed in the source document; they are not alphabetized within the reference list entry. The author listing should end with a period.

One author: **Baker, F. M.**

Two authors: **Baker, F. M., & Lightfoot, O. B.**

Seven or more authors: **Baker, F. M., Lightfoot, O. B., Saxe, G. B., O'Neil, J. M., Egan, J., Henry, W. A., et al.**

Publication Date   Provide, in parentheses, the year the source document was copyrighted or produced. If there is a specific month or month and day, also include that information. Place a period after the closing parenthesis.

(1993).

(1993, September).

(1993, September 15).

(n.d.). Use if no date is available.

Title of Article or Chapter   Capitalize only the first word of the title and subtitle; also capitalize any proper nouns (such as names, holidays, and street addresses) contained in the title or subtitle. Do not italicize or use quotation marks. Capitalize the first word following a colon. Place a period at the end of the title.

Simple title: **Beyond the melting pot.**

Title with subtitle: **Husbands at home: Predictors of paternal participation.**

Periodical:

Deutsch, F. M., Lussier, J. B., & Servis, L. J. (1993). Husbands at home: Predictors of paternal participation in childcare and housework. *Journal of Personality and Social Psychology, 65,* 1154–1166.

Nonperiodical:

O'Neil, J. M, & Egan J. (1992). Men's and women's gender role journeys: Metaphor for healing, transition, and transformation. In B. R. Wainrib (Ed.), *Gender issues across the life cycle* (pp. 107–123). New York: Springer.

Title of Work and Publication Information—Periodicals (anything published on a periodic basis, such as a magazine or newspaper):

- List the full name of the periodical, journal, or magazine in upper- and lowercase letters. Italicize the name of the journal/periodical and the volume number.
- Include the volume number (if present) for journals and other periodicals. Do not use "Vol." before the volume numbers.
- Provide page numbers. Use "p." for a single page, "pp." for multiple pages; use the p./pp. marker only for references to newspapers, *not* in references to journals or magazines.
- Place a comma after the title and after the volume number. Finish the section with a period. Be sure to turn off italics after entering the volume information.

Journal:

Buss, D. M., & Schmitt, D. P. (1993). Sexual strategies theory: An evolutionary perspective on human mating. *Psychological Review, 100,* 204–232.

Magazine:

Henry, W. A., III. (1990, April 9). Beyond the melting pot. *Time 135,* 28–31.

Title of Work—Nonperiodical: Capitalize only the first word of the title and subtitle; also capitalize any proper nouns contained in the title or subtitle. Do not italicize or use quotation marks. Capitalize the first word following a colon. Place a period at the end of the title.

Chapter Title: Capitalize only the first word of a chapter title. Do not italicize or use quotation marks. Place a period at the end of the chapter title.

Book Title: Capitalize the first word of the book title; also capitalize any proper nouns and the first word following a colon. Italicize the book title. Follow the title with parentheses containing the page numbers for the chapter. Place a period at the end of the book title.

Saxe, G. B. (1991). *Cultural and cognitive development: Studies in mathematical understanding.* Hillsdale, NJ: Erlbaum.

Publication Information—Nonperiodicals: Provide the city and state/province or country where the publisher is located. You do not need to provide the state/province/country information if the city is well known and cannot be confused with another location. Follow the location with a colon. Provide the name of the publisher following the colon and end with a period.

Location, ST: Hillsdale, NJ: Erlbaum.

Location/Province/Country: Toronto, Ontario, Canada: University of Toronto Press.

Location, Country: Oxford, England: Basil Blackwell.

Major City: Amsterdam: Elsevier.

Retrieval Information, Electronic Sources Include the date, name, and/or address from which the information was obtained. If your information is obtained from a database, no address is needed. If the retrieval information concludes with an Internet address, you do not end it with a period.

Retrieved August 22, 2005, from http://www.apa.org/ Journals/webref.html
Retrieved August 22, 2005, from the Emerald database.

Nondatabase electronic source:

Benton Foundation. (1998, July 7). Barriers to closing the gap. In *Losing ground bit by bit: Low-income communities in the information age* (chap. 2). Retrieved August 18, 2001, from http://www.benton.org/Library/Low-Income/two.html

Database electronic source:

Eid, M., & Langeheine, R. (1999). The measurement of consistency and occasion specificity with latent class models: A new model and its application to the measurement of affect. *Psychological Methods, 4,* 100–116. Retrieved November 19, 2000, from PsycARTICLES database.

Basic Examples of Reference List Entries Templates The following are general examples of reference list entries taken from the APA manual (p. 225).

Periodical:

Author, A. A., Author, B. B., & Author, C. C. (1994). Title of article. *Title of Periodical, xx,* xxx–xxx.

Nonperiodical:

Author, A. A. (1994). Title of work. Location: Publisher.

Part of a Nonperiodical (book chapter):

Author, A. A., & Author, B. B. (1994). Title of chapter. In A. Editor, B., Editor, & C. Editor (Eds.), *Title of Book* (pp. xxx–xxx). Location: Publisher.

Online Periodical:

Author, A. A., Author, B. B., & Author, C.C. (2000). Title of article. *Title of Periodical, xx,* xxx–xxx. Retrieved month day, year, from source.

Online Document:

Author, A. A. (2003). *Title of work.* Retrieved month day, year, from source.

Pages 232–236 contain a list of various types of source material, along with a section number where a sample reference entry for each source type can be found in the APA manual.

Citing Information

The following must be cited:

- **Direct quotations**—whenever you quote either a person or a printed source, you must cite that source immediately so that there is absolutely no confusion over the origin of the source.
- **Anything that is not common knowledge**—when we speak of common knowledge, keep in mind that we are defining common knowledge as *"common knowledge within the field."* For example, if you were to state in your paper that Whitman invented free

verse, that would be considered common knowledge: Any English major or English instructor should be aware of this well-known fact. Keep in mind, however, that it is always best to err on the side of safety. When in doubt, cite your source.

- **Original ideas, not your own**—if you had the idea first, and then you saw the idea in print, legally it would be all right not to cite it. However, keep in mind that it is best to protect yourself from charges of plagiarism: Cite the source.
- **Summarized material**—if you are summarizing material from a source, you must cite the source.
- **Paraphrased material**—this is the greatest cause of all Honor Code violations. Paraphrasing does not mean that you simply change a couple of words in the original version nor does it mean that you simply substitute synonyms whenever possible. To properly paraphrase a source, the material must be put in your own words. If your material matches the original closely in sentence structure and word choice, you have not paraphrased correctly and could be charged with plagiarism. If you're only changing a few words, quote rather than paraphrase.
- **Statistics**—statistical data not generated by your own research must be cited and the source of the statistics must be clear to readers in the body of your report.
- **Graphics other than clip art**—any graphic material (photographs, line drawings, charts, graphs) that is not clip art and is not of your own making must be cited.

APA STYLE HEADINGS
(APA MANUAL, §§3.31 AND 3.32, PP. 113–115; PP. 289–290)

The easiest way to think about the headings in your paper is to compare them to the levels of an outline, using a combination of Roman numerals, Arabic numbers, and alphabet letters. APA style uses up to five levels of headings; formatting the captions as each level depends on the number of levels the paper contains. In outline terms, the APA heading levels are as follows:

First Level
A. Second Level
  I. Third Level
    a. Fourth Level
      i. Fifth Level

Papers with only one heading level (I.), format the heading caption as follows:

Papers with two heading levels (I., A.) are formatted as follows:

You might also want to check on these websites for additional information.

APA ONLINE RESOURCES

http://owl.english.purdue.edu/workshops/hypertext/apa/index.html
http://humanities.byu.edu/linguistics/Henrichsen/APA/APA02.html
Definitely check out this site: http://www.citationmachine.net/

⓭

NEXT STEP: ACTION RESEARCH

The applied research project is just the beginning. Now that you have completed the literature review process and applied this information to an instructional situation, you have a good foundation to begin action research in your own classroom.

Action research involves a more scientific approach than the applied research project. This type of research is a systematic way of studying what is happening in the school or individual classroom and looking at ways for improvement.

According to the North Central Regional Educational Laboratory (2004), "Action research is inquiry or research in the context of focused efforts to improve the quality of an organization and its performance. It typically is designed and conducted by practitioners who analyze the data to improve their own practice. Action research can be done by individuals or by teams of colleagues. The team approach is called *collaborative inquiry*."

The George Mason University Graduate School of Education, provides an in-depth outline for action research on their site: http://gse.gmu .edu/research/tr/TRaction.shtml

CONCLUSION

PRINCIPLES OF EDUCATIONAL RESEARCH

Several principles must be considered when conducting educational research. These could fall under the categories of:

- Legal
- Procedural
- Moral/Ethical

Legal issues play a role any time that you deal with human subjects. The National Research Act of 1974 was established to regulate research involving people and to ensure that any participants in the study are not put in any mental of physical danger. The following website provides additional information regarding dealing with human subjects and The National Research Act:

http://www.unlv.edu/Research/OPRS/history-ethics.htm

The Family Educational Rights and Privacy (FERPA) act was also passed in 1974. This act ensures confidentiality of all participants in the study. To enforce this confidentially, the Human Subjects Review Board reviews proposals and research to check for violations. The following website provides additional information:

http://www.ed.gov/policy/gen/guid/fpco/ferpa/index.html

Procedure principles must also be considered in action research. When considering a research project for your classroom, you first need to consider if the research is "doable." Can you realistically perform the research taking into consideration the constraints in time, money, and resources?

You also need to consider the simplicity of the research. A simple format and question can add to the reliability and validity. Are you measuring what you state you are measuring? Can the procedure be reproduced? Can the research procedures be accurately followed?

Moral and ethical issues of research deal with the honesty surrounding reporting findings, communicating with participants, and contributing to a needed knowledge base. Even if you do not find what you hoped to find, it is essential that the findings be reported accurately and honestly. Did you communicate with the participants exactly what they were

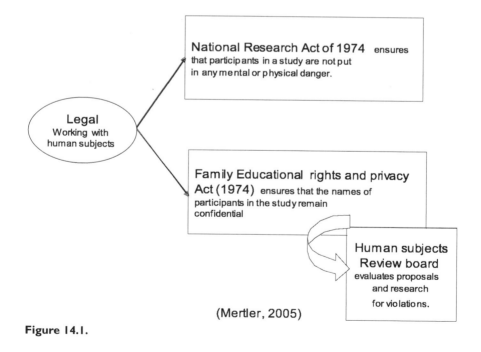

(Mertler, 2005)

Figure 14.1.

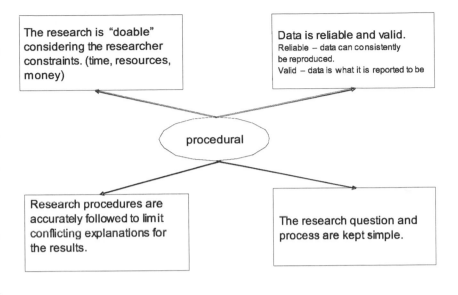

(Mertler, 2005)

Figure 14.2.

to expect? Was the information gleaned beneficial to the general knowledge base? Was your research beneficial?

Applied research offers you an opportunity to practice identifying a topic and synthesizing information. It then guides you through the development of a valuable tool for classroom use. This process can be used to enhance instruction on any level and with any discipline.

Research provides documentation that validates your current practices and leads you into more effective classroom instruction.

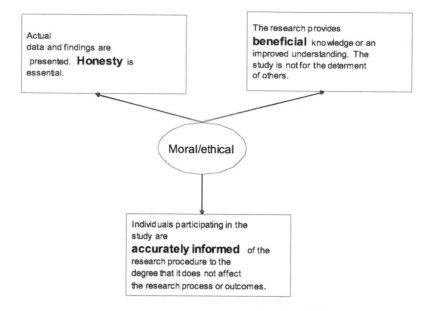

(Mertler, 2005)

Figure 14.3.

APPENDIX A

FRAMEWORK

Applied Research
Organizer

1.Topic

↓

2. Question/Problem

↓

3. Literature Search

↓

4. Product/Application

APPENDIX B
TOPIC ORGANIZER

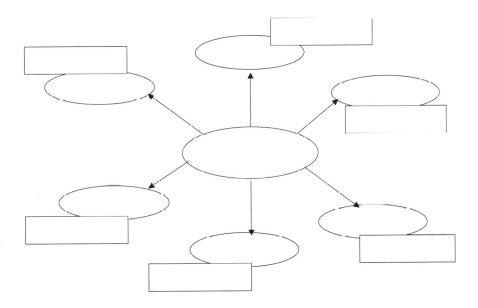

APPENDIX C

SAMPLE APPLIED RESEARCH PROJECT

This portion of the book contains a sample of an actual applied research project. Recently assigned to a third grade classroom, this teacher wants to incorporate children's literature into the math curriculum, specifically in the areas where her students show a weakness.

She starts with the organizer that allows her to identify and narrow the questions. She then focuses on the specific areas that need to be researched in the literature to answer the questions. Based on what she found in the literature, she identifies quality children's trade books and locates strategies for literature and math integration. Using classroom test results she pinpoints the deficient math areas of her students.

Using the literature review findings and the test indicators, this teacher develops an application that uses quality literature and effective instructional strategies for the remediation of third grade math state standard skills (figure C.1).

Using Children's Literature
to Address a Math Skill Deficit
Lynne Fultz
Master of Education Student
July 8, 200x

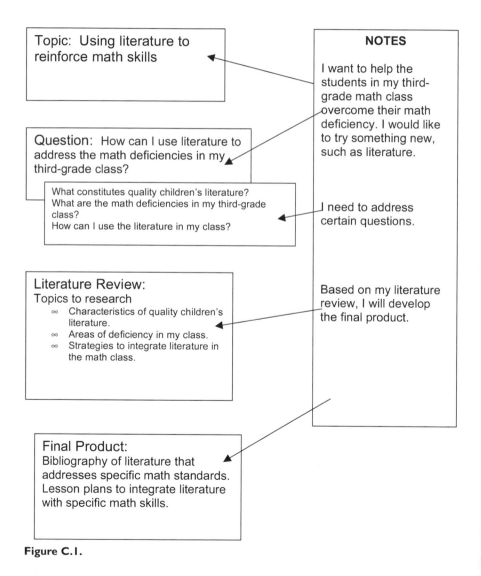

Topic: Using literature to reinforce math skills

Question: How can I use literature to address the math deficiencies in my third-grade class?

What constitutes quality children's literature?
What are the math deficiencies in my third-grade class?
How can I use the literature in my class?

Literature Review:
Topics to research
- ∞ Characteristics of quality children's literature.
- ∞ Areas of deficiency in my class.
- ∞ Strategies to integrate literature in the math class.

Final Product:
Bibliography of literature that addresses specific math standards. Lesson plans to integrate literature with specific math skills.

NOTES

I want to help the students in my third-grade math class overcome their math deficiency. I would like to try something new, such as literature.

I need to address certain questions.

Based on my literature review, I will develop the final product.

Figure C.1.

TABLE OF CONTENTS

INTRODUCTION

Although my third grade class shows an 80-percent pass rate for the mathematics' state standards test, there is still a 20-percent chance that it has not mastered the required skills. This project investigates possible ways to offer remediation by integrating children's literature with specific areas of math deficiency. The following background information and literature review outline the characteristics of quality children's literature, describe effective instructional math practices, and identify the specific areas of deficiency.

The application component of this project provides recommended children's literature with correlating standards and lesson plans for the identified math standards.

RESEARCH QUESTION

How can children's literature be used to address the math deficit in a third grade classroom?

LITERATURE REVIEW

Prior to integrating stories into instruction, teachers need to know what constitutes quality children's literature. "The books we think of as truly excellent have significant content, and if illustrated, fine illustrations. Their total design, from front cover to the final end paper, creates a unified look that seems in character with the content and invites the reader to proceed" (Huck, Hepler, Hickman, & Kiefer, 1997, p. 26).

The American Library Association (1987) lists the qualities of notable children's books "to include books of especially commendable quality, books that exhibit venturesome creativity, and books of fiction, information, poetry, and pictures for all age levels (through age 14) that reflect and encourage children's interests in exemplary ways."

The evaluative criteria used by the American Library Association (1987) includes

- literary quality
- originality of text and illustrations
- clarity and style of language
- excellence of illustration
- excellence of design and format
- subject matter of interest and value to children
- the likelihood of acceptance by children

Literary quality looks at the elements of the story, the setting, point of view, characters, plot, and theme. All of these elements need to be of high quality. For example, the "plot [should] exhibit good development, imagination, and continuity" (Hunsader, 2004, p. 622). The plot also "should have a structure: problem and solution, achievement of a new skill or new experience, or the presentation of an event or an attitude that effects a change in a character or character" (Sutherland, 1997, p. 89). Also, characters are a crucial part of the story and they "must be believable and consistent" (Sutherland, 1997, p. 29). In order for literary quality to be exemplary, all of the elements of the story must come together to attract and hold a child's interest.

The originality of text and illustration need to hold a child's attention. Books should provide readers with new experiences.

When assessing a book for clarity and style of language, a teacher should look at how the ideas of the story are expressed. "Style involves the author's choice of words, the sentence patterns (simple or involved structure, long or short sentences, arrangement of words within the sentences), the imagery used, and the rhythm of the sentences" (Sutherland, 1997, p. 32). Authors use style to set the mood, theme, and suspense, and must be understandable to the children who are reading the book.

When evaluating a book on excellence of illustrations, the illustrations should be "appealing, and representative of a child's perspective" (Hunsader, 2004, p. 622). Illustrations are an important part of children's literature. "Young children respond more easily to visual than auditory stimuli; and although they respond to a story, their first interest often is in the pictures" (Sutherland, 1997, p. 36). The illustrations should be both accurate and "synchronized precisely with the text" (Sutherland, 1997, p. 119).

Design and format encompass not only the type size and page layout but also the illustrations and paper quality (Sutherland, 1997). The illustrations and the text should be appropriate for the child's age level for which the book was written.

Subject matter should be of interest and value to children. Stories need to "captivate readers and keep them racing along from page to page, while having sufficient literary distinction to develop children's taste" (Sutherland, 1997, p. 318). The story needs to be interesting and believable.

Quality literature "must be marked by an engaging story line, beautiful language, and a sense of wonder about the world" (Whiten & Whiten as quoted in White, 2002, para. 5). Hunsader (2004) suggests 6 criteria to simplify evaluating children's literature. The following questions help determine if a book is worth using in the classroom:

1. Does the plot exhibit good development, imagination, and continuity? Are the characters well developed?
2. Does the book contain a vivid and interesting writing style that actively involves the child?
3. Are the book's illustrations and text relevant, appealing, and representative of a child's perspective?
4. Are the book's readability and interest level developmentally appropriate for the intended audience?
5. Do the book's plot, style, and graphics/illustrations complement one another?
6. Does the book respect the reader by presenting positive ethical and cultural value? (Hunsader, 2004, p. 622)

The children's literature to be used should not only be of quality but it should also augment the mathematics instruction as well. Books should only be used if they will enhance the math lesson. Whitin believes "good books enrich our daily living and deepen our appreciation of what it means to view the world mathematically" (2002, para. 2). In order to locate books that are of high literary quality and excellent mathematical content, Hunsader (2004) adapted Schiro's criteria for assessing children's literature to use for mathematics instruction. He recommends the following questions:

1. Is the book's mathematic content (text, computation, scale, vocabulary, and graphics) correct and accurate?
2. Is the book's mathematic content visible and effectively presented?
3. Is the book's mathematic content intellectually and developmentally appropriate for its audience?
4. Does the book facilitate the reader's involvement in and use and transfer of its mathematics?
5. Do the book's mathematics and story complement each other?
6. How great are the resources needed to help readers benefit from the books mathematics? (Hunsader, 2004)

Hellwig, Monroe, and Jacobs (2002) believe quality children's literature can help teach mathematics content. They believe, "Trade books allow students to interact with mathematics in context, helping them draw meaningful connections between experiences in the classroom and life outside the classroom" (Hellwig, Monroe, & Jacobs, 2000, p. 138). Children's literature can also be used to help children build background knowledge.

Children use prior knowledge to build new knowledge; if children do not have this background knowledge, it becomes more difficult to add new information (Woolfolk, 2001, pp. 265–266). To ensure all students have the same information to discuss mathematical problems, teachers can use children's literature to provide a common base for all students. "Literature provides a common experience for every child in the classroom" (Kristo & Giard, 1995, p. 111).

Schiro (1997) states that language allows children to construct meaning (p. 69). Reading children's literature helps students construct meaning for "new experiences" (Schiro, 1997, p. 69). When teachers read a book to their class, the students can "develop shared mathematical understandings with others in their classroom" (Schiro, 1997, p. 71). This will allow students to discuss their shared experience and understandings.

Illustrations in books provide students with a visual connection to the real world (Kolstad, Briggs, & Whalen, 1996). Children often respond to illustrations before they respond to the story (Sutherland, 1997). The illustrations in stories can allow students to make connections they might have missed by just hearing the story.

Although many teachers use children's literature to teach reading or extend language learning, few use it to teach mathematics. This area is many times taught in isolation with no connections to other disciplines. The National Council of Teachers of Mathematics states, "unless connections are made, children will see mathematics as a collection of isolated topics (quoted by Leitze, 1997). Children's literature will allow "the new math skill [to] be associated with the meaningful contexts" (Kolstad, Briggs, & Whalen, 1996, para. 3). Children need to see the mathematical connections to the real world because this stresses the importance of the uses of mathematics and "gives children the opportunity to make sense of mathematics and to gain mathematical power" (National Council of Teachers of Mathematics, 2000, quoted by Moyer).

Literature "involves making meaning as one lives through the literary experiences" (Schiro, 1997, p. 49). "Literature provides the texture for joining the impersonal subject matter and the personal connections to be made by the student" (Bosma & Devries Guth, 1996, p. 7). Allowing students to see connections between math and the real world could give students the motivation to learn mathematics.

Not only can children's literature provide students with real-world connections, it can also enhance mathematical communication skills through discussions of the literature. "Children learn mathematics through the use of language. Mathematics concepts are often tied to the language children use to express these ideas. Opportunities for discourse in both reading and mathematics instruction promote children's oral language skills as well as their ability to think and communicate mathematically" (Moyer, 2000, para. 1).

Students can improve their understanding of math through discussions about the literature they read (Kolstad, Briggs, and Whalen, 1996). Many benefits accompany mathematical discussions. Some of those benefits include "an increased mathematics vocabulary, and a better understanding of the concepts and processes discussed in class"

(Kolstad, Briggs, and Whalen, 1996, para. 38). "Talking promotes understanding" (Huinker & Laughlin, 1996, p. 88). Michael Schiro (1997), author of *Integrating Children's Literature and Mathematics in the Classroom: Children as Meaning Makers, Problems Solvers and Literary Critics* agrees, "When studying mathematics, children learn mathematics through the use of language, whether the language being used by them is everyday language or mathematical language" (p. 67).

Discussions allow students to hear how other students are solving problems through a think-aloud model. "As students talk about their experiences and test their new ideas with words, they become aware of what they really know and what more they need to learn" (Huinker & Laughlin, 1996, p. 81). Discussions also allow children to see that different strategies can be used to solve problems.

When students participate in class discussions about books, they not only talk through their own ideas but they experience learning through listening to their classmates. Students "construct meaning by interacting with peers through discussions in which children use various forms of language (verbal, written, diagrammatic, etc.) to share meanings, clarify thoughts, and test adequacy of understandings related to the book that they are working with" (Schiro, 1997, p. 60).

Many teachers might be unsure of how to use children's literature to teach mathematics. Teachers can have students problem solve in groups and then share their responses with the class. Moyer's (2000) suggestions for using children's literature to teach mathematics are: have students model the story, have students retell the story using equations and illustrations, and have teachers ask students new questions based on the book. Illustrations can also provide a stepping stone between reading the book and class discussions. Teachers can have students look at the illustrations and discuss different problems that can be solved.

This literature review identifies characteristics of quality children's literature and gives an overview of the why and how of using this literature to teach math. The research now must identify the specific areas in math where students show a deficiency. By reviewing previous year's math test scores, five areas of need emerged. These include:

1. Number and Number Sense
2. Computations and Estimation

3. Measurement and Geometry
4. Probability and Statistics
5. Patterns, Functions, and Algebra (Department of Education, 2003).

The Department of Education suggests that the category Number and Number Sense should "promote an understanding of counting, classification, whole numbers, place value, simple fractions, number relationships ("more than," "less than," and "as many as"), and the effects of simple operations on numbers (fact families)" (2002).

For the category of Computation and Estimation, estimation instruction focuses on

- relating the mathematical language and symbolism of operations to problem situations.
- understanding different meanings of addition and subtraction of whole numbers and the relation between the two operations.
- developing proficiency with basic addition, subtraction, and multiplication facts and related fact families.
- gaining facility in manipulating whole numbers to add and subtract and in understanding the effects of the operations on whole numbers.
- developing and using strategies and algorithms to solve problems and choosing an appropriate method for the situation.
- choosing, from mental computation, estimation, paper and pencil, and calculators, an appropriate way to compute.
- recognizing whether numerical solutions are reasonable.
- experiencing situations that lead to multiplication and division, such as equal groupings of objects and sharing equally.
- performing initial operations with fractions and decimals (Department of Education, 2002).

The third category is Measurement and Geometry. Measurement "focuses on developing the skills and tools needed to measure length, weight/mass, capacity, time, temperature, area, perimeter, volume, and money" (Department of Education, 2002). In third grade, students also will "recognize the differences between using nonstandard and standard units of measure" and "simple U.S. Customary and metric units" (Department of Education, 2002).

Geometry focuses on:

- observing, comparing, and investigating three-dimensional objects and their two-dimensional faces.
- sorting objects and ordering them directly by comparing them one to the other.
- describing, comparing, sorting, and classifying shapes.
- exploring symmetry, congruence, and transformation (Department of Education, 200).

The fourth category is Probability and Statistics. "The focus of probability instruction at this level is to help students begin to develop an understanding of the concept of chance" and "They begin to describe the likelihood of events, using the terms impossible, unlikely, equally likely, more likely, and certain" (Department of Education, 200).

The last category is Patterns, Functions, and Algebra. The students "observe, recognize, create, extend, and describe a variety of patterns in the real world" and "they will use patterns to explore mathematical and geometric relationships and to solve problems, and their observations and discussions of how things change will eventually lead to the notion of functions and ultimately to algebra" (Department of Education, 200).

The lowest score for each of the five reporting categories was determined by comparing the results of the three schools to find the question with the lowest percentage of correct responses. When schools did not have the same question with the lowest percentage of correct responses in that reporting category, the percentages for the low-scoring questions of the three schools and the school division were averaged. The lowest percentage was then used to determine the question with the lowest percentage of correct answers for that particular category.

After the questions with the lowest percentage of correct answers were determined, the Mathematics Standards were examined to find the standard that matched the question.

For the reporting category Number and Number Sense, the question with the lowest percentage of correct answers was: identify models of equivalent fractions (Department of Education, 2003). This correlates with the standards for students to compare the numerical value of two fractions having like and unlike denominators, using concrete or picto-rial models involving areas/regions, lengths/measurements, and sets (Department of Education, 200).

For reporting category Computation and Estimation, the questions with the lowest percentage of correct answers was: solve a problem by multiplying a two-digit number and a one-digit number (Department of Education, 200). This correlates with the mathematics standards; the student will represent multiplication and division, using area and set models, and create and solve problems that involve multiplication of two whole numbers, one factor 99 or less and the second factor 5 or less (Department of Education, 2002).

For reporting category Measurement and Geometry, the question with the lowest percentage of correct answers was: identify a reasonable unit for the capacity of a container (Department of Education, 2003). This correlates with the mathematics standards; the student will esti-mate and then use actual measuring devices with metric and U.S. cus-tomary units to measure

1. length—inches, feet, yards, centimeter, and meters.
2. liquid volume—cups, pints, quarts, gallons, and liters.
3. weight/mass—ounces, pounds, grams, and kilograms (cite).

For reporting category Probability and Statistics, the questions with the lowest percentage of correct answers was: solve a problem by interpreting a bar graph with increments of 10 (Department of Education, 2003). This correlates with the mathematics standards; the student will read and in-terpret data represented in line plots, bar graphs, and picture graphs and write a sentence analyzing the data (Department of Education, 200).

For reporting category Patterns, Functions, and Algebra, the ques-tion with the lowest percentage of correct answers was: identify a nu-meric pattern following the same rule as a specific pattern (Department of Education, 2003). This correlates with the mathematics standards; the student will recognize and describe a variety of patterns formed us-ing concrete objects, numbers, tables, and pictures, and extend the pat-tern, using the same or different forms (concrete objects, numbers, ta-bles, and pictures) (Department of Education, 200).

Using these five deficient third grade mathematics standards, lessons were developed to demonstrate how children's literature could be used to teach deficient third grade mathematics.

CONCLUSION

This literature review research has outlined the characteristics of quality children's literature and shown why and how it can be used to teach deficient mathematics skills. The discussion of children's literature was followed by an explanation of the deficit area and how this area was identified as an area that needed improvement. The application portion of this project uses the information provided in the literature review to develop mathematics lessons, using children's literature.

APPLICATION STRAND

Number and Number Sense, Fractions, Grade Level 3
Stage 1: Desired Results

Content Standard   The student will compare the numerical value of two fractions having like and unlike denominators, using concrete or pictorial models involving areas/regions, lengths/measurements, and sets.

Understanding(s)   Students will understand that the denominator tells the number of equal parts in a whole and the numerator tells how many equal-size parts are being considered.

Essential Knowledge   Compare the values of two fractions having like denominators where the denominators are 2, 3, 4, 8, or 10, using concrete or pictorial models. Use the terms *greater than, less than*, or *equal to* or symbols >, <, or = to compare their values. Compare the values of two unit fractions (a fraction in which the numerator is one), having unlike denominators, where the denominators are 2, 3, 4, 8, or 10, using concrete or pictorial models. Use the terms *greater than, less than*, or *equal to* or symbols >, <, or = to compare their values.

Compare the values of two fractions having unlike denominators where the denominators are 2, 3, 4, 8, and 10, using concrete or pictorial models. Use the terms *greater than*, *less than*, or *equal to* or symbols >, <, or = to compare their values.

Students will know/be able to understand that the value of a fraction is dependent on both the number of parts in a whole (denominator) and the number of those parts being considered (numerator).

Stage 2: Assessment Evidence

Performance Tasks   The students will be asked to represent different fractions by shading in different shapes. They will then have to identify the fraction from a given shape.

Other Evidence
Formative:
- Working in pairs the students will manipulative items into fractions.
- Exit ticket

Summative:
- Test

Step 3: Learning Plan

Before the Lesson   Get a pizza box and make two pizzas out of cardboard.

Anticipatory Set   The teacher will read *Pizza Man* by Marjorie Pillar. Ask the students what is their favorite type of pizza? Make a graph on the board:

Pepperoni/Cheese/Sausage/Other

Show the students one of the pizzas. Tell the students that this is one whole pizza. Ask:

- How many slices do you usually get out of one whole pizza?
- If I have four people who want pizza and eight slices how many slices can each person have?

When we divide the pizza and give each person their slices, we are using fractions. The students will do a Think/Pair/Share.

- What is a fraction? (A fraction is a way to represent part of a whole or part of a group.)
- What is the denominator?
- What is the numerator?

Students will then share their answers with the class.

GOAL SETTING INTRODUCTION

On the board, the teacher will put up one of the cardboard pizzas. The teacher will then ask the students, "If you have eight people for dinner, how can we make sure everyone gets an equal amount of pizza?" Discuss.

"Today, we are going to learn how to compare fractions. Remember, a fraction has a numerator and a denominator. A numerator is the top number in a fraction; it tells you how many of those parts you are describing. A denominator is the bottom number of a fraction. You can remember that because it starts with d and down starts with d. The denominator tells you how many equal parts are in the whole."

Input

"Today, you will be making paper plate pizzas. Each of your pizzas will have a different amount of slices." Each student will get six different colored paper plates.

The teacher will tell the students the following instructions while modeling what they are to do.

1. "On your first paper plate (white) write the number 1. This is going to be a whole pizza."
2. "On your second paper plate (red), draw a line down the center. You will now cut along this line. How many pieces do you have?

Hold up one of the pieces you just cut. What is the fraction for the amount you have in your hand? (½) Write ½ on each of the two pieces you just cut. How many halves make a whole? You can put the halves on the whole pizza and you will see that two halves do make a whole."

3. "What would you do if you had one pizza and four friends came over? With the blue paper plate draw a vertical line down the center; draw a horizontal line across the center of the plate. Now cut along the two lines. How many pieces do you have? (4) What fraction is each piece? (¼) How many fourths do you need to make a whole, two halves, and one half?"

4. "Take a green paper plate and watch me as I divide my plate into thirds. Now draw your lines and cut them out. How many pieces do you have? Which is more ¼ or ⅓? Compare ½ to ⅓, which is more? If we wanted to write the number sentence for that, we would write ½ >⅓. > means greater than and < means less than."

5. "Draw a circle on a piece of paper and figure out where you would draw straight lines to make 8 slices for a pizza." Let students come up and demonstrate on the board. After students have demonstrated on the board model drawing the lines in front of the class and then they will draw the lines on the gray paper plate. "What fraction are you going to write on each of your pieces? (⅛) Which is more ⅜ or ¼? How would the number sentence be written?"

6. Have students work in pairs to decide how they would divide their last plate into tenths.

7. Students can draw lines on their plates but cannot cut them out until the teacher looks at their plate. Ask students to label their plate with the correct fraction. (¹⁄₁₀)

Guided Practice Students will work with a partner.

"Using your paper plate pizzas, compare fractions and complete the number sentence on your whiteboard."

Compare ¾_____⁵⁄₁₀

When everyone is done, the teacher will have students hold up their whiteboards so that she can check everyone's answer. The teacher will then provide individual attention to those who are having difficulty.

I will continue having students compare fractions with their white board.

Compare ½ _____ ⅔
Compare ⅝ _____ ¾
Compare ⅒ _____ ⅘
Compare 1 _____ ⁷⁄₁₀

Independent Practice   Each student will create five problems comparing fractions using their pizzas. They will then swap problems with their partner and complete the problems their partner wrote.

Journal Writing

The students will write in their journal. "A fraction is _____. We use fractions in many ways. One way we use fractions is_____."

Closure   The teacher will review what was learned today.

The students will then give an exit ticket. They will draw two squares, shade in a portion of each square, and write the fraction represented for each. They will then write: The numerator is_____.

The denominator is_____.

They will also write a number sentence comparing the two fractions.

Extension

Those students who needed to be challenged should read *Piece=Part= Portion: Fractions=Decimals=Percents* by Scott Gifford. They should then write the decimal on each portion of their paper plate pizzas. Students can compare decimals as well as fractions.

Lesson adapted from *Math Wise!* By Jim Overholt

Materials Needed

- Pizza box
- Two cardboard pizzas
- Six packages of paper plates in different colors
- Tests

Additional Literature

Pizza Man by Marjorie Pillar
Give Me Half! by Stuart Murphy

Fraction Action by Loreen Leedy
Eating Fractions by Bruce McMillan.
Piece=Part=Portion: Fractions=Decimals=Percents by Scott Gifford

STRAND: COMPUTATION AND ESTIMATION

Multiplication and Division, Grade Level 3, Stage 1: Desired Results

Content Standard The students will represent multiplication and division, using area and set models, and create and solve problems that involve multiplication of two whole numbers, one factor of 99 or less and the second factor of 5 or less.

Essential Understandings

- Understand various meanings of multiplication and division
- Understand the effects of multiplying and dividing whole numbers

Students will know/be able to:

- Model multiplication, using area and set models.
- Solve multiplication problems, using the standard multiplication algorithm, where one factor is 99 or less and the second factor is 5 or less.

Create and solve word problems involving multiplication, where one factor is 99 or less and the second factor is five or less.

Stage 2: Assessment Evidence

Performance Tasks

- The students will be asked to write and solve multiplication word problems, where one factor is 99 or less and the second factor is 5 or less.
- The students will solve multiplication problems using the standard multiplication algorithm, where one factor is 99 or less and the second factor is 5 or less.

Other Evidence

Formative:

- Classroom observation
- While working in pairs, students will solve multiplication problems they created with dice
- Word problems students create and solve

Summative:

- Test

Step 3: Learning Plan

Before the Lesson   Number the pages in the book because this will make it easier to locate pages while doing the lesson.

Anticipatory Set   The teacher will ask, "Who can tell me different ways we can count objects?" (2s, 3s, addition, multiplying) Ask the students, "Why do we use multiplication?" (Multiplication is a faster way of counting.)

Goal Setting Introduction   The teacher will tell the students that today they are going to learn how to multiply when they have one factor that has two digits. She will then ask the students, "Can someone give me a factor that has two digits? The second factor we will use is going to be a 5 or less. Write an example of a problem on the board: 23 x 4 = _____."

Input   Before reading the book, the teacher will tell the students they need to raise their hands whenever they hear a math moment. "After reading the book, we will go back and talk about the math moments in the story. Read Amanda Bean's *Amazing Dream: A Mathematical Story* by Cindy Neuschwander. Who can tell me the math moment on page 1? Open the book to page 1 (picture of buildings)." The teacher will ask the students how many windows are on page 1 and 2. (This is a review of multiplication with single digits.) Then she will ask the following questions and let students discuss their answers:

- "How did you figure that out?"
- "What is another way we could figure out how many windows are on these two pages?"
- "How can we check our work?"

(This will be where we begin using a factor with two digits)

- "How many lollipops are on page 2?" (5×4 = ___)
- "What if we had 15 blocks with four lollipops each? How can we figure it out?" The teacher will post an overhead picture of 15 blocks with four lollipops on each.

Then she will write on the board

$$\begin{array}{r} 15 \\ \times 4 \end{array} \qquad 15 \times 4 =$$

The students should try to solve the problem. Then the students will discuss how they came up with the answer.

On the board model:

$$15 \times 4 = (10 \times 4) + (5 \times 4)$$

The teacher will show students how to solve the problem using the standard multiplication algorithm.

She will give students graph paper. The teacher will model this activity on the board while students do it at their seats. The students will make a rectangle 15 squares across by 4 squares down. The students will use a red colored pencil to color 5 rows. This is the one's place value. This will show the students $5 \times 4 = 20$. Using a blue colored pencil, the students will color 10 rows. This is the 10's place value. This will show the students that $10 \times 4 = 40$.

Using the same technique, model another problem on the board. Show the students page 5 in the book. Ask, "How many bushes are in the park? How did you solve this problem?"

The problem is 12×5 = ___. $(10 \times 5) + (2 \times 5) = 12 \times 5$

The teacher will remind the students that $10 \times 5 = 5 \times 10$. Using graph paper, the students will solve the problem.

Guided Practice Students will work in pairs. They will be given three dice and a worksheet.

The teacher will demonstrate with large dice in front of the class.

The first two dice rolled will give the first factor and the teacher will write the numbers in the boxes. The third die will give the last factor. Students will solve the problem using the standard multiplication algorithm method. They will also use graph paper for four of the eight problems. The teacher will walk around the class and observe students at this time. The teacher will provide additional instruction for those students who are experiencing difficulty.

Independent Practice   The teacher will show students page 9 in *Amanda Bean's Amazing Dream: A Mathematical Story* by Cindy Neuschwander. There are 63 books in one bookcase. There are four bookcases. The teacher will have students solve the problem, "How many books are in the library?"

The teacher will tell the students that they are now authors and are going to continue the story of *Amanda Bean's Amazing Dream*. The students will write a multiplication problem using 1 two-digit number and another number that is 5 or less. The students will draw an illustration to go with the problem. The students will solve the problem they write. After the students write and solve their problem, they must solve two of their classmates' word problems.

Closure   The students will choose an index card that has a multiplication problem written on it. The students will demonstrate two different ways to solve the problem and will demonstrate how they check their work.

Additional Literature $7 \times 9 = Trouble$ by Claudia Mills (This would be a good read aloud for the week.)

Materials Needed

- Read *Amanda Bean's Amazing Dream: A Mathematical Story* by Cindy Neuschwander.
- Overhead slide with 15 blocks each having four lollipops
- Dice (Three for each pair)
- Graph paper
- Colored pencils
- Index cards (5×8) with multiplication problems written on them
- Worksheets (2 for each student)
- Test

STRAND: MEASUREMENT AND GEOMETRY MEASUREMENT

Grade Level 3, Stage 1: Desired Results

Content Standard   The student will estimate and then use actual measuring devices with metric and U.S. customary units to measure

- length—inches, feet, yards, centimeters, and meters,
- liquid volume—cups, pints, quarts, gallons, and liters, and
- weight/mass—ounces, pounds, grams, and kilograms

Essential Question(s):

- What two parts does a measurement have? (a number and a unit example: 6 feet)
- What are standard units?
- What are nonstandard units?

Students will know/be able to:

- Identify and use the following units of length: centimeters, meters, inches, feet, and yards.
- Identify and use the following units of liquid volume: cups, pints, quarts, gallons, and liters.
- Identify and use the following units of weight/mass: ounces, pounds, grams, and kilograms.
- Estimate and then measure lengths of objects to the nearest centimeter and meter and the nearest inch, foot, and yard.
- Estimate and then measure the weight/mass of objects to the nearest ounce and pound and the nearest gram and kilogram.
- Estimate and then measure liquid volume to the nearest cup, pint, quart, gallon, and liter.

Stage 2: Assessment Evidence

Performance Tasks   The students will measure one object using as many different units of measurement as possible.
Other Evidence
Formative:

- Teacher observation
- Class discussion

Summative:

- Student's independent work

Step 3: Learning Plan

Anticipatory Set   The teacher will ask the students, "What are some ways in which you can measure objects?" As students brainstorm their ideas, the teacher will write their ideas on the board. The teacher will then ask students, "Why do we need to measure things?" Again, the teacher will write students' responses on the board.

Goal Setting Introduction   The teacher will tell the students, "Today you are going to learn how you can measure different objects using standard and nonstandard units. I am going to read a book about a girl, who finds different ways to measure her dog, Penny. Your job is to find out all the different ways we can measure objects."

Input   Book: *Measuring Penny* by Loreen Leedy

The teacher will read *Measuring Penny*. The students will then discuss the book.

Some questions you might want to ask:

- What other ways could Penny have been measured?
- If you were measuring Penny, what tool would you have used and what would you have measured?
- Did Lisa use standard or nonstandard units when measuring Penny?
- Why do you think Lisa used these standards of measurement?
- What were the ways Lisa measured Penny?
  - Length of Penny's nose—inches
  - Length of Penny's tail—dog biscuits
  - Width of Penny's paw—centimeters
  - Height—inches and feet
  - Weight—seesaw and scale
  - Volume of Penny's food and water—cup
  - Time it takes to take care of Penny—minutes, hours
  - Temperature Penny exercises best—Fahrenheit, Celsius
  - Costs to have a dog—dollars and cents

Guided Practice   The students will work with a partner. Each pair of students will be given an object that they will have to measure using as many different units of measurement as possible. They will write down their units of measurement and the number they came up after measuring their object. The students will then present their object and results to the class. Other students can suggest other ways the pair could measure their object.

The students will write in their math journal: In math today, I learned . . .

Independent Practice   Students will go to 10 different measuring stations and measure objects or answer questions at that station.

- What instrument would you use to measure liquids? (Have different measuring tools at the station for students to look at thermometer, ruler, cup, and scale.)
- How much rice is there? (Put ½ cup of rice in a bowl. Have measuring cups, measuring spoons, ruler, and thermometer at the station.)
- Estimate how much water is in the container?
  - ° One cup
  - ° One pint
  - ° One quart
  - ° One gallon
- Measure the width of the book with nonstandard units (at this station, place a book, tape measure, paper clips, and a pencil).
- Estimate how much the bag of birdseed weighs (put out a five-pound bag of birdseed).
  - ° 1 ounce
  - ° 16 pounds
  - ° 5 pounds
  - ° 4 ounces
- Estimate how much water the watering can can hold.
  - ° 2 teaspoons
  - ° 2 cups
  - ° 2 gallons
- Measure the yarn in inches and centimeters (tape a piece of yarn to the desk and have a ruler at the station).
- The length of the dog from nose to tail is closest to (have a picture of a dog on the table and a row of paper clips underneath the picture).
  - ° 6 paper clips
  - ° 8 paper clips
  - ° 10 paper clips
  - ° 15 paper clips

- Use a centimeter ruler to answer this question. What is the height in centimeters of the birdbath in the picture (have a picture of a birdbath on the table)?
- Which is closest to the size of your hand?
  ° 12 centimeters
  ° 10 centimeters
  ° 11 centimeters
  ° 9 centimeters

Closure   The students will complete an exit ticket and tell me which tool they will use to measure an object and why they chose that tool.

Additional Literature

- *Measuring Penny* by Loreen Leedy
- *Jim and the Beanstalk* by Raymond Briggs
- *How Big Is a Foot?* by Rolf Myler
- *How Tall, How Short, How Faraway* by David A. Adler

Materials Needed

- *Measuring Penny* by Loreen Leedy
- Objects for students to measure (cup, soda bottle, bowl of water, dog bone, candy bar, etc.)
  ° rulers
  ° thermometer
  ° measuring cup
  ° scale
  ° rice
  ° bowl
  ° book
  ° tape measure
  ° paperclips
  ° pencil
  ° measuring spoons
  ° yarn
  ° picture of a dog
  ° picture of a birdbath

STRAND: PROBABILITY AND STATISTICS

Graphing, Grade Level 3,
Stage 1: Desired Results

Content Standard   The student will read and interpret data represented in line plots, bar graphs, and picture graphs and write a sentence analyzing the data.

Understanding(s)   Data sets can be analyzed to provide different kinds of information.

Students will know/be able to:

- Read the information presented on a simple bar or picture graph (e.g., the title, the categories, the description of the two axes, the key).
- Read information presented in line plots.
- Analyze and interpret information from simple picture and bar graphs, with data points limited to 16 and categories to 4, by writing at least one statement.
- Analyze and interpret information from line plots, with data points limited to 16, by writing at least one statement.
- Describe the categories of data and the data as a whole (e.g., data were collected on four types of eggs—scrambled, fried, hard boiled, and egg salad— eaten by students).
- Identify parts of the data that have special characteristics, including categories with the greatest, the least, or the same (e.g., most students prefer scrambled eggs).
- Select a correct interpretation of a graph from a set of interpretations of the graph, where one is correct and the remaining three are incorrect.

Stage 2: Assessment Evidence

Performance Tasks

- Students will answer questions based on the information given in a graph.
- Students will make a line graph.
- Students will make a bar graph.

Other Evidence
Formative: Observation/student work
Summative: Test

Step 3: Learning Plan

Before the Lesson   The teacher will put a piece of paper over the title of the book and cover all the graphs in the book with paper. Before the lesson, she will make a graph using student birthdays.

Anticipatory Set   The teacher will ask the students if they have ever been to the zoo. "What kinds of animals live in the zoo?" She will show the students the cover of the book, *Tiger Math: Learning to Graph from a Baby Tiger* (the title should be covered up). "What is the animal on the cover?" After the students identify the animal as a tiger, the teacher will ask them what they know about tigers and write their responses on the board.

Goal Setting Introduction   The teacher will tell the students: "Today we are going to learn about tigers. You will also learn how we can use information to make graphs and how to read graphs."

Input   She will first read the book, *Tiger Math: Learning to Graph from a Baby Tiger*, by Ann Whitehead Nagda and Cindy Bickel and let students absorb the story. Then the students will discuss the story. The teacher will reread the story. This time, the students will listen for things they can graph. The teacher will stop at each page and discuss the graphs.

- Page 8—Picture Graph
  ° The students will tell the teacher what information is on the graph.
  ° What is being graphed?
  ° Which group of tigers is the least?
  ° How many Sumatran tigers are in the wild?
  ° What does each tiger stand for?
- Page 10—Pie Chart. The pie chart shows . . .
- Page 12—What questions can this picture graph answer?

Guided Practice   The students will be put into groups of three. The teacher will put a picture of the graph on page 14 on the overhead.

The students will answer the following question:

How many more pounds did T.J. weigh at 10 weeks than he did at 6 weeks?

The students will share their responses and tell the class how they reached their decision.

On page 16, Students will look at the graph and decide how much heavier Matthew was at 6 weeks than T.J. was at 6 weeks.

The students will be given graph. They will then make a line graph using the following information:

Age in Weeks	Weight
0	3 lbs.
2	5½ lbs.
4	7 lbs.
6	10 lbs.
12	14 lbs.
13	16 lbs.

Independent Practice The teacher will ask the class their favorite color, favorite food, favorite subject in school, favorite season, and birthday month. Students will then use this information to make a bar graph. They will label both axes. Students will make up a question their classmates can answer based on the graph the student made. These graphs will be put on an interactive bulletin board and students will solve the problems.

Closure "Use the birthday graph you made before the lesson." Students will have to answer two of the four questions about the graph and make up one question that can be answered using the graph.

- How many children have birthdays in July?
- Which month has the most birthdays?
- Which month has the least birthdays?
- How many more students have birthdays in January than in December?

Materials Needed

- Graphing Assessment
- *Tiger Math: Learning to Graph from a Baby Tiger* by Ann Whitehead Nagda and Cindy Bickel

STRAND: PATTERNS, FUNCTIONS, AND ALGEBRA

Grade Level 3, Patterns, Stage 1: Desired Results

Content Standard   The student will recognize and describe a variety of patterns formed using concrete objects, numbers, tables, and pictures, and extend the pattern, using the same or different forms (concrete objects, numbers, tables, and pictures).

Essential Understanding(s)

- The student will use problem solving, mathematical communication, mathematical reasoning, connections, and representations to
- Recognize repeating and growing numeric and geometric patterns (e.g., skip counting, addition tables, and multiplication tables).
- Describe repeating and growing numeric and geometric patterns formed using concrete objects, numbers, tables, and/or pictures, using the same or different forms.
- Extend repeating and growing numeric and geometric patterns formed using concrete objects, numbers, tables, and/or pictures, using the same or different forms.

Students will know/be able to:

- Understand that numeric and geometric patterns can be expressed in words or symbols.
- Understand the structure of a pattern and how it grows or changes.
- Understand that mathematical relationships exist in patterns.
- Understand that patterns can be translated from one representation to another.

Stage 2: Assessment Evidence

Performance Tasks   The students will locate patterns in the book and also locate patterns in the world around them.

Other Evidence:

Formative: The students will make and continue patterns on whiteboards.

Summative: The students will continue patterns already started.

Step 3: Learning Plan

Before the lesson:

- Cover the title and words of the book.

Anticipatory Set:

- Take a picture walk of *Math Counts Pattern* by Henry Pluckrose.

The students will look at pictures of zebras, peacocks, and other items that have patterns. The students will describe what they see. For example, the zebra has black and white stripes. The teacher will then ask the students, "What can you tell me about the stripes? Many of the things around us have patterns. Can you tell me about any other things you can think of that have patterns?"

Goal Setting Introduction

"Today, we are going to learn more about patterns. Patterns can be made with numbers, shapes, and colors. Patterns can repeat but they can also grow. Today, we are going to learn about different kinds of patterns."

Input 1   Review repeating patterns before teaching students patterns that grow.

The teacher will ask the students, "Who can give me an example of a pattern?" The teacher will put a pattern on the board. "In kindergarten, first, and second grade, you learned about repeating patterns." The teacher will put a repeating pattern on the board. "What are some repeating patterns you remember making?" AB, AABB, ABC . . .

"In the book we read, what type of pattern does the zebra have?"

Guided Practice 1   The students will be given die cut shapes in different colors. The teacher will ask students to make an AB pattern (this should be a review). The teacher will demonstrate an AB pattern with magnetic die-cut shapes. The students will make patterns on their desk with the die-cut shapes, AABB, ABC, AABBCC, ABB. Students will take turns doing their patterns on the board.

Input 2   The teacher will demonstrate number patterns on the board (for example, 2, 4, 6, 8). The teacher will model how to figure out the rule for the pattern. The teacher will write a number pattern on the board: 3, 6, 9, 12. The teacher will let students discuss the pattern with a neighbor to see if they can locate the rule for the pattern. The students will then share their answers and tell the class how they came up with the answer. The teacher will model out loud how she solves patterns. The teacher will put another example on the board for students to try to figure out the rule so that they can determine the next number.

Guided Practice 2   The students will be given whiteboards. The students will make number patterns on the whiteboard. The teacher will ask for volunteers to come and put their patterns on the board. The teacher will walk around and assess students' patterns while the class tries to solve the pattern on the board and determine the rule for the pattern (by having students work with whiteboards, students who need to be challenged can devise more complicated patterns).

Independent Practice   The teacher will write patterns on the board and the students will try to continue the pattern and identify the rule.

Triangle, triangle, square, triangle, triangle, square, _____

5, 10, 15, 20,_____What is the rule?

10, 8, 6, _____ What is the rule?

1, 4, 7, 10,_____ What is the rule?

Red, yellow, blue, green, red, yellow,_____

Draw lines—two tall, one short, two tall, _____

If the pattern in the table continues, how many tires must be ordered for 10 cars?_____ What is the rule?

If the pattern in the table continues, how many tires must be ordered for 5 tickets?_____ What is the rule?

Closure   The teacher will have students recap what they learned today. She will write their responses on the board.

Materials Needed

- *Math Counts Pattern* by Henry Pluckrose
- Die-cut shapes
- Whiteboards
- Whiteboard markers
- Socks (to erase whiteboards)
- Paper

Additional Literature:

Math Counts Pattern by Henry Pluckrose

A String of Beads by Margarette S. Reid

Patterns by Sara Pistoia

Table C.1.

Math Standard	Correlating Children's Literature
The students will read and write six-digit numerals and identify the place value of each digit.	*On Beyond a Million: An Amazing Math Journey* by David M. Schwartz *One in a Billion* by Michael McGaffe & Diane Gard
The students will round a whole number, 999 or less, to the nearest ten, hundred, and thousand.	*On Beyond a Million: An Amazing Math Journey* by David M. Schwartz *One in a Billion* by Michael McGaffe & Diane Gard
The students will compare two whole numbers.	*On Beyond a Million: An Amazing Math Journey* by David M. Schwartz *One in a Billion* by Michael McGaffe & Diane Gard
The students will recognize and use the inverse relationships between addition/subtraction and multiplication/division to complete basic fact sentences.	*Mission Addition* by Loreen Leedy *7 x 9 = Trouble* by Claudia Mills
The students will a) divide regions and sets to represent a fraction and b) name and write the fractions represented by a given model (area/region, length/measurement, and set). Fractions (including mixed numbers) will include halves, thirds, fourths, eights, and tenths.	*Fraction Action* by Loreen Leedy *Piece = Part = Portion: Fractions = Decimals = Percents* by Scott Gifford *Eating Fractions* by Bruce McMillan
The students will compare the numerical value of two fractions having like and unlike denominators.	*Fraction Action* by Loreen Leedy
The students will read and write decimals expressed as tenths and hundredths, using concrete materials and models.	*Piece = Part = Portion: Fractions = Decimals = Percents* by Scott Gifford
The students will solve problems involving the sum or difference of two whole numbers, each 9,999 or less, with or without regrouping using various computational methods, including calculators, paper and pencil, mental computation, and estimation.	*Math for All Seasons* by Greg Tang *The Shark Swimathon* by Stuart Murphy
The students will recall the multiplication and division facts through the nine tables.	*Each Orange Had 8 Slices: A Counting Book* by Paul Giganti *Sea Squares* by Joy Hulme *Amanda Bean's Amazing Dream: A Mathematical story* by Cindy Neuschwander *One Grain of Rice* by Demi *Math for All Seasons* by Greg Tang *Too Many Kangaroo Things to Do!* by Stuart Murphy *The Best of Times* by Greg Tang *7 x 9 = Trouble* by Claudia Mills *One Hundred Hungry Ants* by E. Phinczes

(continued)

Table C.1. (*continued*)

Math Standard	Correlating Children's Literature
The students will represent multiplication and division, using area and set models.	*The Doorbell Rang* by P. Hutchins *Anno's Magic Seeds* by Mitsumasa Annon *The Greatest Guessing Game: A Book about dividing* by Robert Froman *Division* by Sheila Cato *7 x 9 = Trouble* by Claudia Mills
The students will add or subtract with proper fractions having like denominators of 10 or less.	*Fraction Action* by Loreen Leedy
The students will add and subtract with decimals expressed in tenths.	*Fraction Action* by Loreen Leedy *The Big Buck Adventure* by Shelley Gill & Deborah Tobola
The students will determine by counting the value of a collection of bills and coins, whose total value is $5.00 or less, compare the value of the coins or bills, and make change.	*The Monster Money Book* by Loreen Leedy *Alexander, Who Used to be Rich Last Sunday* by Judith Viorst *The Penny Pot* by Stuart J. Murphy *Fraction Action* by Loreen Leedy *The Big Buck Adventure* by Shelley Gill & Deborah Tobola *How the Second Grade Got $8,205.50 to Visit the Statue of Liberty* by Nathan Zimelman *Pigs Will Be Pigs* by Amy Axelrod
The students will estimate and then use actual measuring devices with metric and US customary units to measure	*Measuring Penny* by Loreen Leedy *Jim and the Beanstalk* by Raymond Briggs *How Big Is a Foot* by Rolf Myler *How Tall, How Short, How Faraway* by David Adler
The students will tell time to the nearest 5-minute interval and to the nearest minute using analog and digital clocks.	*Pigs on a Blanket* by Amy Axel
The students will identify equivalent periods of time including relationships among days, months, and years, as well as minutes and hours.	*Math Counts Time* by Henry Pluckrose
The students will read the temperature to the nearest degree from a Celsius thermometer and a Fahrenheit thermometer.	*Temperature and You* by Betsy and Giulo Maestro
The students will analyze two-dimensional and three-dimensional geometric figures.	*Sir Cumference and the First Round Table: A Math Adventure* by Cindy Neuschwander *Sir Cumference and the Sword in the Cone: A Math Adventure* by Cindy Neuschwander
The students will identify and draw representations of line segments and angles, using a ruler or straightedge.	*Angles Are Easy as Pie* by Robert Froman *Shape Up! Fun with Triangles and Other Polygons* by David Adler

Table C.1. (continued)

Math Standard	Correlating Children's Literature
TSW, given appropriate drawings or models, will identify and describe congruent and symmetrical, two-dimensional figures.	*What Is Symmetry?* by Mindel and Harry Sitomer
The students will a) collect and organize data b) construct a line plot	*Tiger Math: Learning to Graph from a Baby Tiger* by Ann Whitehead Nagda and Cindy Bickel
The students will read and interpret data	*Tiger Math: Learning to Graph from a Baby Tiger* by Ann Whitehead Nagda and Cindy Bickel
The students will investigate and describe the concept of probability	*Betcha!* by Stuart J. Murphy
The students will recognize and describe a variety of patterns	*Math Counts Pattern* by Henry Pluckrose *A String of Beads* by Margarette S. Reid *Patterns* by Sara Pistoia

REFERENCES

Adler, D. (1998). *Shape up! Fun with triangles and other polygons*. New York, NY: Holiday House.

Adler, D. (1999). *How tall, how short, how faraway*. New York, NY: Holiday House.

American Library Association. Children's notable books: Terms and criteria. Retrieved online February 21, 2004. http://www.ala.org/ALSCTemplate.cfm?Section=childrensnotable&Template=/ContentManagement/ContentDisplay.cfm&ContentID=52296

Anno, M. (1995). *Anno's magic seeds*. New York, NY: Philomel Books.

Axelrod, A. (1994). *Pigs will be pigs*. New York, NY: Simon & Schuster Books for Young Readers.

Axelrod, A. (1996). *Pigs on a blanket*. New York, NY: Simon & Schuster Books for Young Readers.

Bosma, B., & DeVries Guth, N. (1995). Making connections. In B. Bosma & N. Devries Guth (Eds.), *Children's literature in an integrated curriculum: The authentic voice* (pp. 1–13). New York, NY: Teachers College Press.

Briggs, Raymond. (1970). *Jim and the beanstalk*. New York, NY: The Putnam & Grosset Group.

Cato, S. (1998). *Division*. Minneapolis, MN: Carolhoda Books.

Demi. (1997). *One grain of rice*. New York, NY: Scholastic Press.

Franke, M. (1996). Fostering young children's mathematical understanding. C. Howe (Ed.), *Teaching 4- to 8-year-olds* (pp. 93–112). Baltimore, MD: Paul H. Brookes.

Froman, R. (1975). *Angles are easy as pie.* New York, NY: Thomas Y. Crowell.

Froman, R. (1978). *The greatest guessing game: A book about dividing.* New York, NY: Thomas Y. Crowell.

Gifford, S. (2003). *Piece=part=portion: Fractions=decimals=percents.* Berkley, CA: Tricycle Press.

Giganti Jr., P. (1992). *Each orange had 8 slices.* New York, NY: Greenwillow Books.

Gill, S., & Tobola, D. (2002). *The big buck adventure.* Watertown, MA: Charlesbridge Publishing.

Haury, D. (2001). *Literature-based mathematics in elementary school.* Eric Clearinghouse for Science and Environmental Education. [ED 464 807]

Hellwig, S., Monroe, E., & Jacobs, J. (2000). Making informed choices: Selecting children's trade books for mathematics instruction. *Teaching Children Mathematics.* V7 no. 3.

Huck, C., Hepler, S., Hickman, J., & Kiefer, B. (1997). *Children's literature in the elementary school.* Madison, WI: Brown & Benchmark Publishers.

Huinker, D., & Laughlin, C. (1996). Talk your way into writing. In P. Elliott & M. Kenney, (Eds.) *Communication in mathematics, K-12 and beyond.* Reston, VA: National Council of Teachers of Mathematics.

Hulme, J. (1991). *Sea squares.* New York, NY: Hyperion Books for Children.

Hunsader, P. (2004). Mathematics trade books: Establishing their value and assessing their quality. *The Reading Teacher.* V57 no. 7.

Hutchins, P. (1986). *The doorbell rang.* New York, NY: Greenwillow Books.

Kellough, R. & Roberts P. (2002). *A resource guide for elementary school teaching planning for competence.* Upper Saddle River, NJ: Prentice-Hall.

Kolstad, R., Briggs L., & Whalen, K. (1996). Incorporating language arts into the mathematics curriculum: Literature survey. *Education.* V116 no. 3 Retrieved from Infotrac October 10, 2003.

Kristo, J., & Giard, M. (1995). A sense of balance: A first grade literature connection. In B. Bosma & N. Devries Guth (Eds.), *Children's literature in an integrated curriculum* (pp. 110–127). New York, NY: Teachers College Press.

Leedy, L. (1992). *The monster money book.* New York, NY: Holiday House.

Leedy, L. (1994). *Fraction Action.* New York, NY: Holiday House.

Leedy, L. (1997). *Measuring Penny.* New York, NY: Henry Hold and Co.

Leedy, L. (1997). *Mission Addition.* New York, NY: Holiday House.

Leitz, A. (1997). Connecting process problem solving to children's literature. *Teaching Children Mathematics* v3 no. 7. Retrieved September 4, 2003 from Infotrac database.

Lewis, B., Long, R., & Mackay, M. (1993). Fostering communication in mathematics using children's literature. *Arithmetic Teacher*. V40.

Maestro, B., & Maestro, G. (1990). *Temperature and you*. New York, NY: Dutton Children's Books.

McMillan, B. (1991). *Eating Fractions*. New York, NY: Scholastic.

Mills, C. (2002). *7 x 9 = trouble*. New York, NY: Farrar Straus Giroux.

Moyer, P. (2000). Communicating mathematically: Children's literature as a natural connection. [Electronic Version]. *The Reading Teacher*, v54, no. 3.

Murphy, S. (1996). *Give Me Half!* New York, NY: HarperTrophy.

Murphy, S. (1996). *Too many kangaroo things to do!* New York, NY: HarperCollins.

Murphy, S. (1997). *Betcha!* New York, NY: HarperCollins.

Murphy, S. (1999). Learning math through stories. *School Library Journal*. v5 no. 3. Retrieved October 7, 2003 from Wilsonweb.

Murphy, S. (2001). *The shark swimathon*. New York, NY: HarperCollins.

Myler, R. (1962) (1990). *How big is a foot?* New York, NY: Random House Children's Books.

Nagda, A., & Bickel, C. (2000). *Tiger math: Learning to graph from a baby tiger*. New York, NY: Henry Holt and Company.

National Council of Teachers of Mathematics (2000). Standards for grades pre-K–2. Retrieved September 8, 2003 from http://standards.nctm.org/documents/chapter4/index.htm

Neuschwander, C. (1997). *Amanda bean's amazing dream: A mathematical story*. New York, NY: Scholastic Press.

Neuschwander, C. (1997). *Sir cumference and the first round table: A math adventure*. Watertown, MA: Charlesbridge.

Neuschwander, C. (2003). *Sir cumference and the sword in the cone: A math adventure*. Watertown, MA: Charlesbridge.

Overholt, J. (1995). *Math wise! Hands-on activities and investigations for elementary students*. West Nyack, NY: The Center for Applied Research in Education.

Pillar, M. (1990). *Pizza Man*. New York, NY: HarperCollins.

Pinczes, E. (1993). *One hundred hungry ants*. Boston, MA: Houghton Mifflin.

Pistoia, S. (2003). *Patterns*. Chanhassen, MN: The Child's World.

Pluckrose, H. (1995). *Math counts pattern*. Chicago, IL: Children's Press.

Pluckrose, H. (1995). *Math counts time*. Chicago, IL: Children's Press.

Reid, M. (1997). *A string of beads*. New York, NY: Dutton Children's Books.

Schiro, M. (1997). *Integrating children's literature and mathematics in the classroom: Children as meaning makers, problem solvers, and literary critics*. New York, NY: Teachers College Press.

Schwartz, D. (1985). *How much is a million?* New York, NY: Lothrop, Lee & Shepard Books.

Schwartz, D. (1999). *On beyond a million: An amazing math journey.* New York, NY: Doubleday Book for Young Readers.

Sitomer, M., & Sitomer, H. (1970). *What is symmetry?* New York, NY: Thomas Y. Crowell Company.

Sutherland, Z. (1997). *Children & books.* New York, NY: Addison Wesley Longman.

Tang, G. (2002). *Best of times.* New York, NY: Scholastic Press.

Teppo, A. R. (Ed.), (1999). NCTM standards documents. *Reflecting on practice in elementary school mathematics: Readings from NCTM's school-based journals and other publications.* (pp. 6–7) Reston, VA: The National Council of Teachers of Mathematics.

Viorst, J. (1978). *Alexander, who used to be rich last Sunday.* New York, NY: Macmillian.

Virginia Department of Education. (2002). *Virginia standards of learning assessments: Spring 2002 released test; Grade 3 mathematics.* Richmond, VA: Author.

Virginia Department of Education. (2002). *Mathematics standards of learning: Curriculum framework; Grade 3.* [Electronic Version] Retrieved Online May 23, 2004 from http://www.pen.k12.va.us/VDOE/Instruction/Math/grade3math cf.doc. Richmond, VA: author.

Virginia Department of Education. (2003). *Virginia standards of learning assessments: Student performance by question; School report spotsylvania county.* Richmond, Va: Author.

Whitin, D. (2002). The potentials and pitfalls of integrating literature into the mathematics program [Electronic Version]. *Teaching Children Mathematics,* v8, no. 9.

Williams, R. (2001). *The coin counting book.* Watertown, MA: Charlesbridge.

Woolfolk, A. (2001). *Educational Psychology.* Needham Heights, MA: A Pearson Education Co.

Zimelman, N. (1992). *How the second grade got $8,205.50 to visit the Statue of Liberty.* Morton Grove, IL: Albert Whitman.

REFERENCES

Bardine, B. (1997, June). Teacher Research: Getting started. Research to practice. *Ohio Literacy Resource Center*.

Cin, S. T. S., & Williams, J. B. (2006, March). A theoretical framework for effective online course design. *Journal of Online Learning and Teaching* (2/No1).

Dewey, J. (1938/1997) Experience and education. Kappa Delta Pi. Touchstone: New York.

George Mason Graduate School of Education (2005). The process of teacher research. Retrieved January 2007 from http://gse.gmu.edu/research/tr/TRprocess .shtml

Johnson, R. B., & Christensen, L. (2006, October 6). Educational research (glossary). Retrieved February 2007 from http://www.southalabama.edu/coe/ bset/johnson/dr_johnson/2glossary.htm

Laskowski, L. (2000, July 21). Overcoming speaking anxiety in meetings and presentations. Retrieved in February 2007 from the All-Biz.Com Network at http://www.all-biz.com/default.aspx?RelId=33637&issearch=laskowski

Leedy, P. D. (1997). Practical research: Planning and design (6th ed). Upper Saddle River, NJ: Prentice-Hall/Merrill, pp. 71–72.

Mertler, C. A., & Charles, C. M. (2005). Introduction to educational research. 5th edition, Allyn & Bacon/Boston.

Newman, K. A. (1997, February). Combining standards with changing teacher needs: Introducing teacher research strategies to preservice teachers. Paper presented at the 1997 Annual Meeting of the American Association of Colleges for Teacher Education.

North Central Regional Educational Laboratory (2004) Action research. Retrieved January 31, 2007 from http://www.ncrel.org/sdrs/areas/issues/envrnmnt/drugfree/sa3act.htm

Wikipedia Foundation, Inc. (2007, February 2) Peer review. Retrieved February 2007 from http://wikipedia.org/wiki/Peer_review

ABOUT THE AUTHOR

Suzanne Houff is associate professor of education at the College of Graduate and Professional Studies of the University of Mary Washington. She has worked on both an elementary and middle-school level as a classroom teacher and as a library media specialist. After completing her doctorate from Old Dominion University, she moved into higher education and now instructs pre-services teachers as they work toward initial licensure and a master's degree in education.